ATLAS
OF
L✺ST
CITIES

ATLAS
OF
L✳ST
CITIES

A Travel Guide to
Abandoned and Forsaken
Destinations

AUDE DE TOCQUEVILLE

Illustrations
KARIN DOERING-FROGER

BLACK DOG
& LEVENTHAL
PUBLISHERS

ACKNOWLEDGMENTS:

This work is based on an idea by Gérard and Virginie Grandval,
to whom we express our heartfelt thanks.

Black Dog & Leventhal Publishers
Hachette Book Group
1290 Avenue of the Americas
New York, NY 10104
www.hachettegroup.com
www.blackdogandleventhal.com

Printed in Korea
Original interior design by Karin Doering-Froger, with revisions and cover design by Red Herring Design.

IM

First Edition: April 2016

10 9 8 7 6 5 4 3 2 1

Black Dog & Leventhal Publishers is an imprint of Hachette Books, a division of Hachette Book Group.
The Black Dog & Leventhal Publishers name and logo are trademarks of Hachette Book Group, Inc.
The Hachette Speakers Bureau provides a wide range of authors for speaking events. To find out more, go to www.HachetteSpeakersBureau.com or call (866) 376-6591.

ISBN: 978-0-3163-5202-4

CONTENTS

EUROPE

ASIA

INTRODUCTION

"The catalog of forms is infinite. For as long as forms have yet to find their city, new cities will continue to be born. The end of the city begins at the point where forms exhaust their variety and come apart."

—Italo Calvino, *Invisible Cities*

One November day on my way back from Agra, the city famous for the Taj Mahal, I stopped off at Fatehpur Sikri. At the gates of this city built by a Mughal emperor in the sixteenth century, the tumultuous din of Indian life melted away and the bare stones were engulfed by silence. I was struck by the spatial harmony, by the refined architecture of the palaces, courtyards, and terraces, which are all of the same pink color, by the mineral purity of this city perched on a hill at the heart of an immense plain. My thoughts then turned to those who had once invested these walls with life: Akbar, the universal thinker and founder of Fatehpur Sikri, conversing with Jesuit priests in the main courtyard; the women of the harem leaning over their balconies to watch the sun go down; the guards dozing in gloomy recesses. On a large door of Mughal design I came across some calligraphic inscriptions executed by artist-philosophers. One of them proclaimed: "The world is nothing but a footbridge. Cross over without stopping to erect your house there." During the course of my stroll, I became enchanted by this city that time, in depriving it of its perfumes and wall hangings, had rendered more beautiful still.

How to explain the magic of Fatehpur Sikri? How to explain the magic of an abandoned city? Fond as I am of cities, which can be seen as open worlds in a state of perpetual metamorphosis, I am even fonder of dead cities, where the imagination can run free. For the very reason that somewhere no longer exists, it can be transformed into the ideal city, the city of one's dreams. Like fictional characters, cities are born and develop. They undergo various cycles before dying and are eventually resurrected beneath our feet. While passing through Fatehpur Sikri, I discovered a tomb of overwhelming beauty. This wonderful confection of white marble, mother-of-pearl, and ebony wood had been made for Akbar's personal adviser and embodies the emperor's lifelong veneration of a man who had taught him wisdom. For a moment, history commingled with my wandering thoughts. The lost city is thus poetry, dream world, and a setting for our passions and meanderings, a kind of metaphor for our lives. While our fascination with lost cities derives largely from the way they mirror our own existence, there is sometimes another reason: they also attest to the folly of the world, to the violence of nature and the violence of mankind. Here, poetry and reverie play no part. What we feel is simply bewilderment at that which is beyond our control. Such is the case with cities that are destroyed while bustling with activity, entombed beneath the debris of war or swept away by a nuclear blast, victims of destruction individual or collective, natural or historical. I cannot help wondering about the motivation of the busloads of tourists who pass through Pripyat, which was evacuated in haste following the Chernobyl nuclear disaster. Are they fascinated by the misfortune that can befall a place—unique like ourselves and also, like ourselves, capable of being wiped out in an instant? From what obscure depths does this empathy with disaster spring? Human beings are complex creatures. These cities that suffer a tragic fate have one thing in common: they all inevitably return to nature, giving rise to the poignant sight, whether at Pripyat or Agdam, Kantubek or Kadykchan, of vegetation forcing its way between stones, cracking asphalt, and smothering misshapen beams. Nature takes its revenge, showing how cities can be extinguished as suddenly as shooting stars.

Happily, most lost cities have known a gentler kind of existence, their histories unfolding over several millennia. Belying the inscription at Fatehpur Sikri, no sooner did mankind begin to settle in one place than he raised his house, constructing places of exchange and creativity in a variety of forms—trading centers, medieval cities protected by ramparts, capitals of the arts during the Renaissance, industrial cities in the nineteenth century—settlements glorious or vulnerable, born of chance, of a need for protection, of ambition, each one with its own history, images, and fate, which could be the departure of a king, the end of a civilization or era, or the failure of a project.

Some cities have had a number of lives, one such being Bam, which was repeatedly rebuilt over the course of the centuries and, having been devastated by an earthquake, is now defying the desert all over again. In ancient times cities were the result of a drawn-out cycle of construction and destruction. This is perhaps why their history pervades the walls long after the city has been abandoned. "Alas, the shape of a city changes faster than the human heart," lamented Baudelaire. For those antique settlements built with an eye on other, pre-existing cities, similarities abound, for example Rome's multiple satellite cities scattered around the perimeter of the Mediterranean. And yet Mari, Leptis Magna, and Pompeii each have their own individual charms deriving from the patch of earth on which they are built and the luminosity of the skies above. Strolling across the paving stones of Djémila, at the heart of a landscape of mountains and ravines, how can the visitor not be bewitched by these stones that evoke a sense of the eternal at the heart of an Algeria that has been given a rough ride by history? I also experienced that magic moment when the past imposes itself on the space around us, in Yemen, where I was on the trail of Henri de Monfreid. One morning I visited Ma'rib, which lies on the edge of a desert so dry that it smells of dust. Of this city that was once an important halt on the Incense Road, nothing remains but a heap of ruins watched over by goats. A little boy appeared from nowhere and, taking me by the hand, led me to a dilapidated wall. There he showed me a stone bearing an inscription in Sabaean. Suddenly these ruins took on a new dimension, assuming the colors and decoration of a time before the opening up of the maritime route brought about the demise of the land route. When a city disappears, a part of history dies with it. To rediscover its traces is to bring this past back to life. Our fascination with these lost cities perhaps stems from some ingrained detective instinct. Each birth is a surprise and each death an enigma, as demonstrated by the brief and frenzied adventure of Sanzhi and Wanli in Taiwan, which sprang from the minds of developers crazy about futuristic design; by Seseña in Spain, which died before it had had chance to live, thanks to the megalomania of one man; and by the somewhat surreal Jeoffrecourt, a mock city dumped in the middle of the Picardy plain as a location for urban guerilla warfare exercises and about whose birth and death it is impossible to be certain as it does not actually exist. Telling their story took me on an adventure. Discovering these places brought home to me that the demise of a city is just as momentous an event as its emergence, and even more importantly that a city is as much a mental space as a physical one: on the one hand it shapes our innermost beings; on the other we make it the object of our fantasies.

When the torch of a Shi Cheng diver resurrects a stone lion submerged under the waters, when a little boy points out a Sabaean inscription, we are transported all of a sudden to a different time, one that is simultaneously beyond time. We are liberated from all ties and are moved to find in this secret beauty the echo of our unaccomplished lives.

DJÉMI

ALGER

ATLANTIC
OCEAN

AFRICA

MEDITERRANEAN SEA
ARTHAGE
TUNISIA
LEPTIS MAGNA
LIBYA
ANTINOË
EGYPT
INDIAN OCEAN
NOVA CIDADE DE KILAMBA
ANGOLA
KOLMANNSKUPPE
NAMIBIA

EGYPT · 27°50′N, 30°50′E

ANTINOË

IN MEMORIAM

"On the first day of the month of Hathor in the second year of the two hundred and twenty-sixth Olympiad," writes Marguerite Yourcenar in her novel *Memoirs of Hadrian*, the beautiful Antinous, Emperor Hadrian's beloved, drowned in the waters of the Nile. It is the autumn of A.D. 130 and the emperor is visiting the Roman province of Egypt. The day on which Antinous drowns is also the "anniversary of the death of Osiris, the god of the dying," an occasion ritually celebrated with an outpouring of tears and lamentation. Was it an accident? Suicide? Tradition has it that the ephebus was sacrificed in order to preserve his royal lover from a dire prophecy. The drama unfolded some five hundred kilometers upstream from Alexandria, "not far from a semi-abandoned pharaonic temple." Hadrian immediately decided to transform this sanctuary into a "place of pilgrimage for all Egypt" in order to ensure that Antinous—assimilated with Osiris—would be venerated in the Greek manner "with games, dancing, and ritual offerings."

Yourcenar describes how Hadrian led his architects along the stony hills, explaining his plan for the construction of an outer wall forty-five stadia (more than seven kilometers) long, and marked out the position of the triumphal arch in the sand.

This is how the city of Antinoë, dedicated to

A place of pilgrimage

for all Egypt

Osiris-Antinous, the last of the Egyptian gods, revered throughout the Roman Empire until the advent of Christian civilization, sprang into life. Prospering on the tax on merchandise destined for Rome, the city remained the administrative center of Middle Egypt until its destruction by the Arabs in 619. Never to rise again, the once prosperous city shrank to the size of a modest village (the present-day El-Sheikh Ibada) on whose outskirts the almost intact triumphal arch and the tall portico of a theater could still be admired by the scholars on Napoleon's 1799 expedition to Egypt.

By the time the Dijonnais archaeologist Albert Gayet undertook an investigation of the site a century later, there was nothing left. The stones had been reduced to lime and employed in the construction of sugar factories or used to fertilize the fields. Gayet describes the remains of the city in his notebooks: "on the shores of the Nile and bordering the desert [...] straddling both plain and desert, [the city] describes a vast parallelogram whose traces can still be discerned, beneath the accumulation of sand stopped by the city walls, at the foot of the stony hills that hug it to the east. Between these hills and the ancient ramparts extends an arid zone a kilometer wide on average, giving no hint of the presence here of antique tombs."

MEDITERRANEAN SEA
ALEXANDRIA
PORT SAID
ISRAEL
CAIRO
NILE
SINAI
ANTINOPOLIS
LIBYAN
DESERT
RED SEA
NILE
NUBIA
EGYPT
LUXOR

For almost twenty years, the archaeologist labored—with passion for his discoveries and bitterness at his chronic lack of resources—to uncover from the sand what he described as an Egyptian Pompeii. First of all there was the famous temple of Ramesses II, whose inscription designating Isis by the near-homonym "Henti-nou-an" provided, he believed, the key to Hadrian's act.

This was followed by the excavation of the enormous, simultaneously Egyptian, Greco-Roman, and Christian necropolis surrounding the temple, from where he extracted a multitude of mummified corpses and a veritable treasure trove of costumes and fabrics dating from the Byzantine era. Gayet dreamed of opening a museum in Paris dedicated to the site. In the meantime, he exhibited his finds in the museum designed and opened by his friend Émile Guimet, thereby triggering a short-lived craze for all things Byzantine around 1900. More concerned, however, with presenting his finds in a lyrical manner than with scientific rigor, Gayet had a tendency to mix together different places and periods, and, to the

An Egyptian Pompeii rising out of the sands

great regret of the researchers who pored over the forty mummies and five thousand objects and textiles that now lie long forgotten in the stores of the Louvre, he failed to adequately document his discoveries. In 2003 a group of Italian archeologists resumed rigorous research at the site—now covered over again by sand, concealing all but a few temples (including that of Ramesses) and sections of wall. Despite the disappearance of Gayet's excavation notebooks, they are trying to restore Antinoë to the state it was in at the beginning of the twentieth century.

In 2012, by means of modern ground-penetrating radar and magnetometry, the researchers set about precisely mapping the city without any digging. This led to the discovery of a long-buried ancient wharf. Unfortunately, their work was interrupted by the recent political disturbances. As things stand today, with the remains threatened by pillaging and systematic destruction in order to extend both the village and the fields, the future of this city born of tragedy remains highly uncertain.

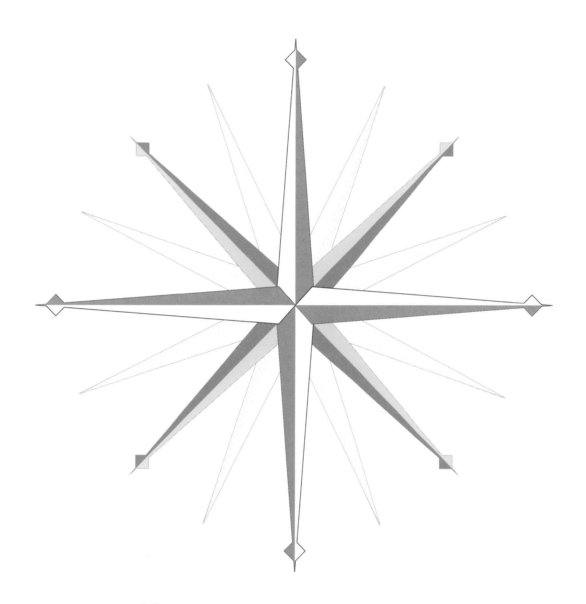

Antinoë remained the administrative center of Middle Egypt until its destruction by the Arabs in 619

TUNISIA · 36°51′N, 10°19′E

CARTHAGE
CARTHAGO DELENDA EST

"Carthage must be destroyed." This famous phrase attributed to Cato the Elder encapsulates almost to the point of caricature the unshakeable desire of the Romans to crush their great rival. Scattered today around the modern city of Tunis, the remains of ancient Carthage give little indication of the power of a city that for centuries defied Rome and dominated the Mediterranean. The best way to gain a sense of its former glory is to read Flaubert. Having immersed himself in the ancient texts and spent time in Tunis acquiring a feel for the place, in his book *Salammbô* the writer tells of the revolt of the barbarian mercenaries employed by the Carthaginians during the First Punic War. In keeping with the fashion of the day, Flaubert paints a picture of a highly sensual Orient. If the work is novelistic in style, however, the facts on which it is based are very real and describe the bellicose destiny of the city that Strabo nicknamed the "ship at anchor." This image seems extremely apt when one stops to consider the geography of Carthage, which was founded in 814 B.C. on a peninsula almost entirely surrounded by the sea on one side and a lake on the other and only connected to the continent of Africa by an isthmus. Almost inevitably, its history is intimately bound up with the water and in particular the Mediterranean Sea, which was the main focus of attention in the ancient world. According to the latest hypothesis, Carthage was founded by Phoenician colonists from Tyre, the Phoenicians being skillful navigators and prodigious traders. Before long, the newly established trading center grew so powerful on the back of maritime commerce that it outdid its mother city. From the sixth century B.C. onward, thanks to its monopoly on maritime relations with

the Orient, it expanded continuously, to Tripolitania in one direction and the Atlantic on the other, forming alliances with the Etruscans and then the Romans. At its peak between the fifth and sixth centuries B.C., this city of almost four hundred thousand inhabitants dominated the sea and played a leading political, economic, and religious role in the ancient world.

This was not at all to the liking of Rome, whose initial relations with Carthage had nevertheless been peaceable, and thus the historic rivals became mortal enemies. From 264 B.C., the antagonism between the two powers was played out in the Punic Wars, the background to Hannibal's brilliant strategy. After more than a century of steadily increasing tensions, the hostilities culminated in the siege of Carthage in 146 B.C. The city defended itself heroically for three years but in the end was completely destroyed by the Romans. Rebuilt by its new occupants, it remained a cultural and religious center after the Roman Empire started to go into decline in the middle of the third century, and until the seventh century was regarded as a promised land by Germanic and subsequently Byzantine and Arab invaders.

Dismembered in the ninth century, the ancient site now displays few signs of its former glory. The massive outline of the Cathedral of St. Louis, built on the site where Louis IX of France was presumed to have died during the Eighth Crusade, seems somewhat out of place among the ruined walls shaded by cypresses. As for the view of the sea hemmed by mountains, it is spoiled by the inescapable presence of modern Tunis. To rediscover the ancient Phoenician trading city, a better course of action would be to lose oneself in old maps—or else to reread Flaubert.

SEBKHET
ARINA

CARTHAGE

TUNIS

LAKE
TUNIS

GULF OF TUNIS

MEDITERRANEAN
SEA

FOREST
OF RADÈS

ALGERIA · 36°18′N, 5°44′E

DJÉMILA
A ROMAN BEAUTY

For Albert Camus, Djémila is the perfect metaphor for the indissolubility of death and the splendor of the world. In *Noces* (Nuptials), he sees this city of the ancient kingdom of Numidia as a "great cry thrown out by the lugubrious and solemn stones at the mountains, the sky, and the silence." The city, claims the writer, is inhabited by the wind alone, which "pounces fitfully on the remains of the houses, on the immense forum that extends from the triumphal arch to the temple." The artist's sense is clear: the precipitous landscape of the southern Atlas Mountains lends the grandiose ruins a tragic air, making the site one of the most enthralling places in the entire region.

The triumphal arch described by Camus was more or less all that was visible of the ancient city when the Duke of Orléans stopped off there in 1839, before Djémila had been excavated. Filled with admiration, the prince wanted to have the monument transported back to Paris. Although this project was abandoned, for reasons unknown, it led to an initial exploration of the ruins. A century passed, however, before proper excavations, facilitated by the construction of a long, winding road providing access to the site, were undertaken. These digs enabled archaeologists to finally uncover the history of Djémila. This history is doubly fascinating, first because of its longevity. Founded in around A.D. 96, this city, which originally bore the Berber name of Cuicul and which testifies to the might of the Severan dynasty of the second century A.D., was in turns Roman, Christian, Vandal, and Byzantine. And second because it is situated on a narrow plateau bordered by ravines, at the intersection of the roads from Sétif to Constantine and from the sea to Aurès, and therefore offers a rare example of the adaptation of Roman town planning to a mountainous environment. Strolling today among the parched vegetation and paved streets delineated by colonnades, the story of the city's development can be read like an open book: to the north, the first city, ramparted against belligerent local tribes and centering on a still impeccably paved forum where the large temple of the capitol rubs shoulders with the curia and the basilica; next, outside the original walls, a second forum, luxurious thermal baths, and, built into the slopes of a hill, a three-thousand-seat theater. In the third century the city numbered some ten thousand inhabitants, who can be imagined going about their business, perambulating from their *domus* to the temples and the two covered markets, whose counters are still in place. In the fourth century a final, Christian, district was added, with two churches and, most conspicuously today, a remarkably well-preserved circular baptistery decorated with mosaics.

What brought about Cuicul's downfall remains a mystery. Broken statues, evidence of a fire, and the absence of precious metals among the ruins suggest the city may have been pillaged. However, in the seventh century Cuicul must still have been an impressive sight, for the newly arrived Muslims renamed it Djamila, the "fair," and respectfully abstained from building there. Algerian historians complain that our own era has fewer scruples. They are currently trying to protect Djémila from unforeseen peril: a major music festival held each year among the ruins.

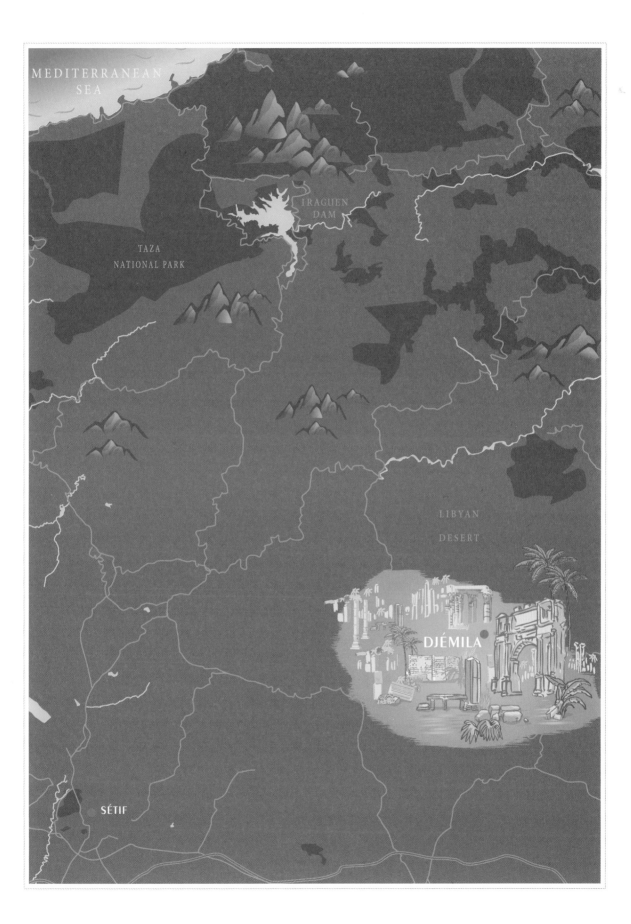

NAMIBIA · 26°41′S, 15°14′E

KOLMANNSKUPPE
ENTOMBED IN SAND

Be warned: do not venture into this city if you are afraid of ghosts. Terrified travelers claim to have encountered the spirits of the dead flitting through its abandoned houses, which disappear a little deeper under the sand each day. Located a few kilometers from the port of Lüderitz, the only inhabited city within a 130-kilometer radius, Kolmannskuppe is *the* place to see in the Namib Desert. However, would-be visitors have to apply for the appropriate permit, which is issued on an individual basis. Without this magic key, there is no hope of entering the 26,000-square-kilometer desert zone, which is bordered by the Atlantic Ocean and extends from Lüderitz in south-western Namibia to Oranjemund, at the border of South Africa, for it is out of bounds to the general public. The reason for this is purely economic: the ground contains diamond deposits, and the authorities therefore choose to keep the area under close control. Indeed the city of Kolmannskuppe (Kolman-skop in Afrikaans) would not have existed but for the diamonds that made it prosperous—and were responsible for its decline.

In 1908, when what is now Namibia was the German protectorate of South-West Africa, a black worker employed on the construction of the railroad between Keetmanshoop and Lüderitz casually picked up a stone that turned out to be a diamond.

Diamonds made it prosperous . . . and were responsible for its decline

As soon as the news got out, people flocked to the place. Amid the frenzy, a new town popped out of the ground like a mushroom. Within the space of a few years it had become one of the most prosperous in Africa. Connected to Lüderitz by a tramway, Kolmannskuppe had its own casino, theater, schools, swimming pool, businesses, and a department store selling all the latest goods from Berlin. It even had a hospital that was one of the first on the continent to be equipped with an X-ray machine! The most select merchandise was imported from Germany and France, and water, which was more expensive in Namibia than beer, was shipped in at great cost. It should be remembered that money was no problem, and it is even said that the streets were swept every day in order to clear them of the sand that obstinately returned on the wind. However, all the commodities and comforts of this colonialist paradise, this "little Germany," were reserved for the engineers and managers of the German company to whom exclusive rights of extraction had been granted. The black workers who did the toughest jobs were housed with their families on a separate site or, if single, accommodated in dormitories. The First World War, which saw the administration of South-West Africa pass to South Africa under a League of Nations mandate, made no impact on the prosperity of Kolmannskuppe. At its peak in the

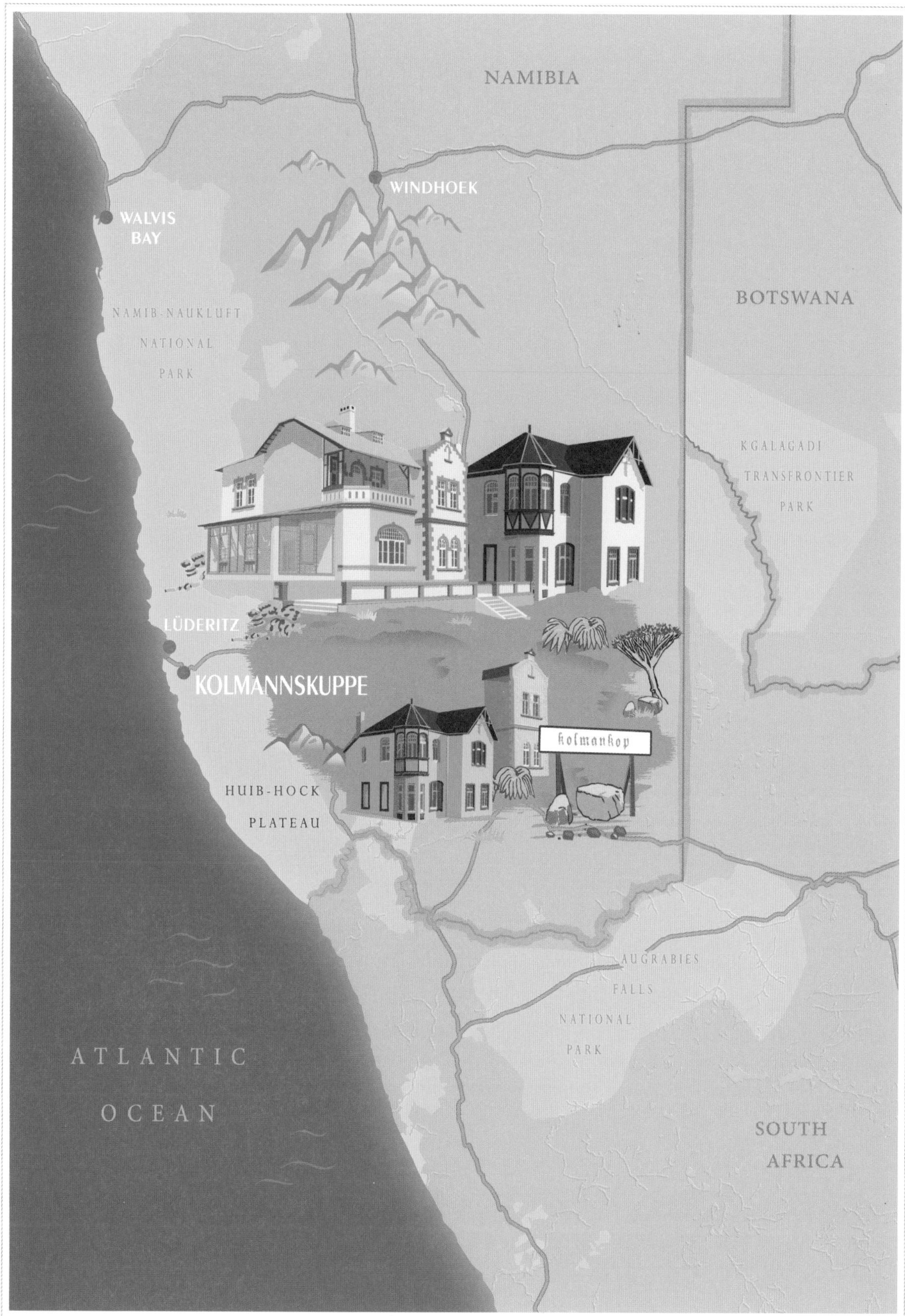

NAMIBIA
WINDHOEK
WALVIS BAY
NAMIB-NAUKLUFT NATIONAL PARK
BOTSWANA
KGALAGADI TRANSFRONTIER PARK
LÜDERITZ
KOLMANNSKUPPE
kolmankop
HUIB-HOCK PLATEAU
AUGRABIES FALLS NATIONAL PARK
ATLANTIC OCEAN
SOUTH AFRICA

1920s, the town boasted more than one thousand inhabitants, almost three hundred of them European. During the following decade, times were less good: adversely affected by the discovery of new deposits in the Oranjemund region and an ensuing fall in price, the former "pearl of the desert" declined as its diamond seams dried up. The end was close. Gradually the population drifted away, although it was not until 1956, the year the hospital closed for good, that the last remaining residents packed their bags and left.

Once deserted, the township sank into oblivion until 1990, when the Namibian government and the De Beers company, partners in the exploitation of the prohibited zone, decided to turn it into a tourist site. The idea was a good one: the buildings emerging from the dunes, the wooden façades faded by the sun, and the interiors invaded by the sands transformed the place into one of southern Namibia's major attractions. Guides were trained to tell visitors about

From 1956

the population

gradually drifted away

and the town sank

into oblivion, leaving time

and the sandstorms

to do their work

the history of the town and a small museum was established in the former casino, where precious stones could also be bought as souvenirs. This return of life to Kolmannskuppe in no way detracts from the strangeness of the place, however. A number of houses have been restored and refurnished in the simultaneously elegant and functional style of the Wilhelminian era, giving the impression they might have been abandoned yesterday. Others have been preserved exactly as their occupants left them, with wallpaper and pictures still clinging to the walls, with baths and kitchens still in place, with counters still visible in the stores and machinery in the workshops— only with everything having been exposed to the ravages of time and sand. Everything here is as if locked into an eternal process of gradual decay, and it is difficult not to succumb to the ambiguous charms of this aesthetic of chaos.

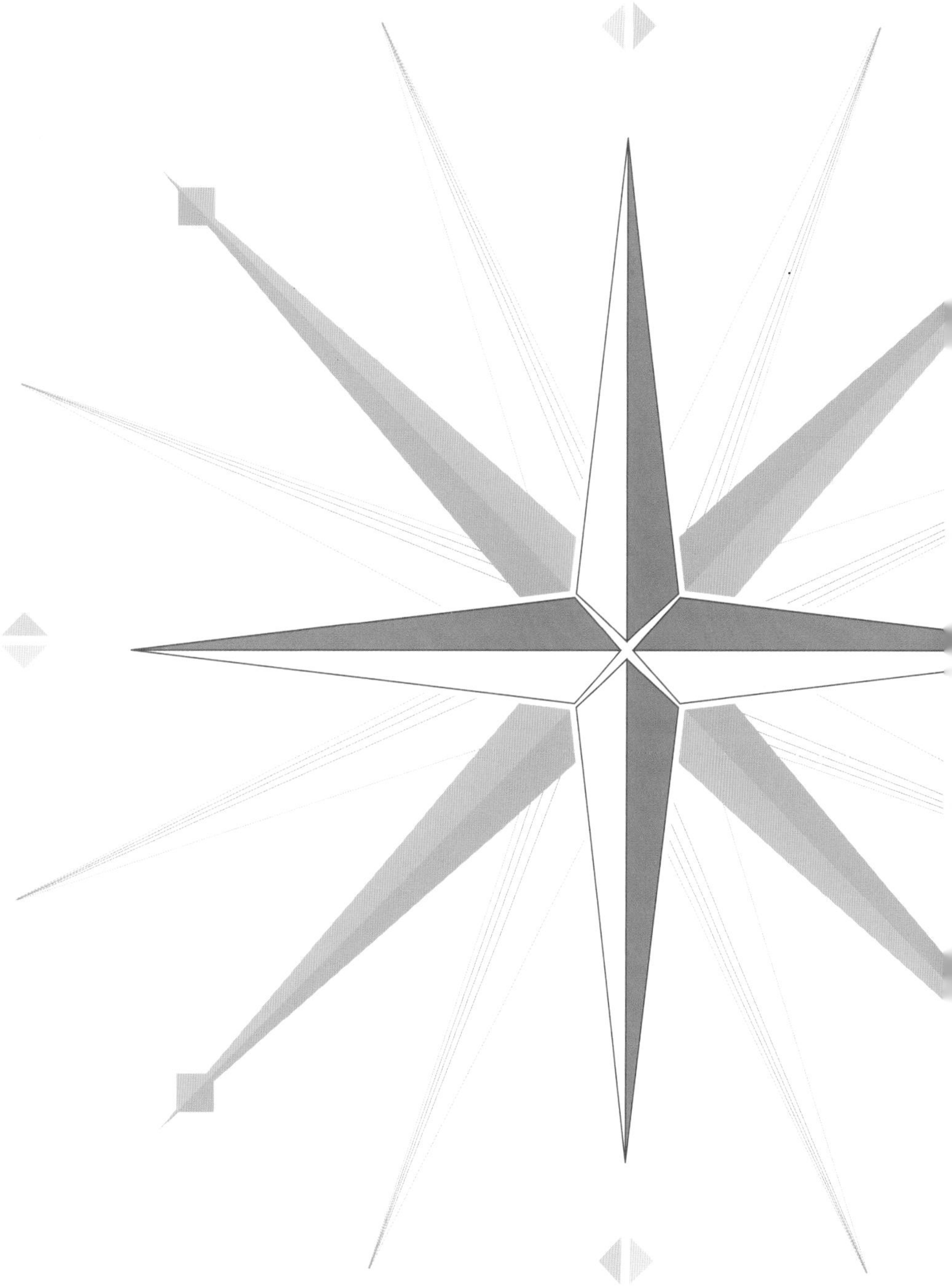

*The Namibian government
has transformed a no-go zone
into a tourist site*

LIBYA · 32°37′N, 14°18′E

LEPTIS MAGNA
THE ROME OF THE SANDS

One hundred and twenty-five kilometers east of Tripoli, not far from the city of Al Khums, the site of Leptis Magna seems utterly indifferent to the troubles rocking present-day Libya.

For centuries, this city founded by the Phoenicians was as powerful—thanks to one of its sons, the Roman emperor Septimus Severus—as Carthage and Alexandria. It was called Magna (the great) in order to distinguish it from Leptis Minor in Tunisia, and its imposing port made it one of the most important Roman colonies on the Mediterranean coast. It was exempt from property tax, and its land prices were as high as in Italy. When Septimus Severus became emperor in A.D. 193, Leptis Magna was embellished with monuments proclaiming the might of a glorious empire. These helped to uphold the city's reputation until the third century, when the city fell into a slow decline. A century later, this decline was sealed by the attacks of Moorish invaders from abroad. When the Roman-Christian world went up in flames in the fifth century, Vandal hordes led by Genseric flooded into Tripolitania. As the master of all Africa, Genseric reorganized the region, retaining Roman law at the heart of his new code and taking Leptis under his control, but with Carthage as the new capital. In 534 the Vandal kingdom was broken up by the Byzantines when they reconquered the whole of North Africa. Leptis Magna once again became the capital of Tripolitania, with reinforced walls but devoid of people.

Weakened by the Vandal conquest and Arab raids, the city dwindled in size. Apart from the port and the old forum, it was more or less deserted. In 642 the demoralized Byzantines were unable to withstand a wave of Arab attacks. This marked the end of a world: Roman civilization vanished from Africa for good, there was a revival of nomadism, and the remains of Leptis Magna sank into the sand.

Hundreds of years later, the ancient capital was to be resurrected in a most unusual way. In the seventeenth century, the presence of blocks of marble scattered all over the site began to attract keen interest from certain quarters. The French consul in Libya, diplomat Claude Lemaire, was a man of few scruples who turned the recovery of the old stones into a veritable industry. Hastily removed, the marble was shipped to Malta, Constantinople, London, or Paris and then carved up like so much raw material and sold to the contractors in charge of the major building sites of the day—with a few exceptions, including the altar of the church of Saint Germain des Prés in Paris and the rood screen of Rouen Cathedral, which are graced by whole columns from Leptis. In the

> *For several centuries, Leptis Magna was as powerful as Carthage or Alexandria*

MEDITERRANEAN

SEA

AL KHUMS

LEPTIS MAGNA

Windsor Great Park, in England, a Roman temple was fabricated from columns and lintels that had been offered to the prince regent, the future King George IV, in 1816. After gathering dust in the British Museum, these remains were clumsily erected by Sir Jeffry Wyatville some ten years later. In 1920 a team of Italian archaeologists (the country had become an Italian colony in 1911) embarked on the first ever excavations of Leptis Magna to be conducted in a scientific manner. As a curious aside, Benito Mussolini was inspired by the former glory of the ancient city to travel there in 1926 and again in 1937. Photographs show Il Duce standing against a backdrop of columns, hands on hips, contemplating the grandeur of Rome, "our model," or perhaps pondering how archaeology could be put to the service of politics.

After the proclamation of independence in 1951, Libya opened its doors to further archaeological expeditions from abroad, while at the same time training its own people in the management of its national assets—mineral as well as cultural, with the discovery of oil fields at the end of the 1950s bringing wealth to the young republic.

Leptis Magna gradually emerged in all its splendor: towering up by the side of the city's paved roads are its extraordinary amphitheater (the largest in North Africa); the Temple of Serapis; the Arch of Septimius Severus, with its fine sculptural decoration; Villa Silin, a magnificent country house that looks out across the sea; and the market, warehouses, and workshops that testify to the commercial dynamism of the Roman era.

In 2011 Irina Bokova, the director-general of UNESCO, urged the military forces engaged in Libya to spare the archaeological remains, which had been declared a World Heritage Site in 1982, so that when peace finally returns to the country, visitors will once again be able to let their imaginations wander against the backdrop of the African Rome. So far, her plea has been respected.

Until the third century A.D., Leptis Magna was considered the "African Rome"

LEPTIS MAGNA
GOLDEN AGES

Ever since antiquity, various cities have symbolized the golden ages of the different civilizations—whether Muslim, Chinese, Indian, or, in the case of Leptis Magna (the "African Rome"), Greco-Roman. The city of Uruk in Mesopotamia, dating from the fourth millennium B.C., is believed to have been the earliest of these city-states. This is where sculpture in the round and writing are believed to have been invented. In India, the inscriptions of Ashoka (304–232 B.C.), the third emperor of the Mauryan dynasty, bear witness to the nonviolent reign of a monarch who conquered most of the Indian subcontinent before converting to Buddhism. In the second century A.D., Palmyra opened its gates to caravans traveling between India and the Roman Empire. After the fall of Petra in Jordan, this oasis in the middle of the Syrian Desert rose to prosperity on the back of trade, the scale of which is demonstrated by the city's ruins. In China the Song dynasty (tenth to thirteenth centuries) transformed its capital, Hangzhou, into a hub of Afro-Eurasian trade, thereby relativizing the importance of the West in the history of the world.

ANGOLA · 8°50′S, 13°16′E

NOVA CIDADE DE KILAMBA

THE PROMISE OF A BETTER FUTURE

Whom should we believe? The foreign journalists whose verdicts of failure on this pharaonic project are all over the Internet? Or the president of the municipality of Kilamba, who in September 2013 declared that all the apartments in the new city had been sold and that by 2015 some sixty to seventy thousand people would be living there (a figure set to increase as subsequent phases of construction come on stream)? The truth may lie somewhere in between, although the suspicion lingers that those who claim that Kilamba is nothing but a ghost town may have some ulterior motive.

It is worth pointing out that this city created out of nothing approximately thirty kilometers south of the Angolan capital, Luanda, bears the stain of original sin as it was constructed in its entirety by a Chinese state-owned enterprise, the China International Trust and Investment Corporation (CITIC). This has not gone down well with the country's traditional trading partners—overwhelmingly European—who are furious at having missed out on lucrative reconstruction contracts following years of destructive civil war. Despite the fact that Luanda, the country's largest city, has not yet managed to rid itself of its belt of enormous shantytowns, the regime of President José Eduardo dos Santos robustly defends the project, an audacious and hitherto unheard of financial arrangement under which the $3.5 billion works have been paid for by deliveries of petroleum from the country's extensive reserves. Since 2010, Angola has been China's number one supplier of crude, ahead of Saudi Arabia. Critics of the new city, however, point to the cost of the apartments, set at between $120,000 and $200,000, a real aberration in a country in which two-thirds of the population live on less than two dollars per day.

It cannot be denied that Kilamba, whose symmetrically laid out apartment blocks extend for tens of kilometers in soulless lines, share the same defects as any metropolis newly risen from the ground—starting with the absence of vegetation, despite the touches of color provided by patches of grass laid out between the buildings. The apartment buildings, resembling immense Lego blocks, are dazzlingly white, and each is covered by a small roof with a gentle slope that could be mistaken from a distance for expertly folded paper. It is important to recognize, however, that in a country ravaged by a protracted civil war, this modern city, which is to be provided with elementary schools, stadia, public parks, malls, and hospitals, and where every home has piped drinking water, can look like an El Dorado to a population thirsty for progress. This city in the making is filled not with ghosts, but with the hope of a better tomorrow.

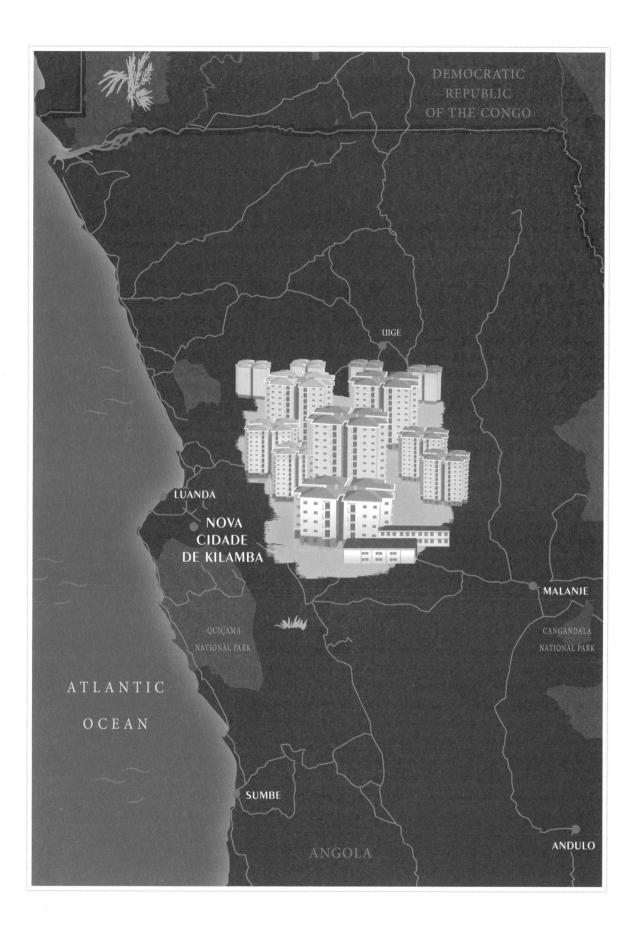

DEMOCRATIC
REPUBLIC
OF THE CONGO

UIGE

LUANDA

**NOVA
CIDADE
DE KILAMBA**

MALANJE

QUIÇAMA
NATIONAL PARK

CANGANDALA
NATIONAL PARK

ATLANTIC

OCEAN

ANGOLA

SUMBE

ANDULO

ARCTIC

OCEAN

GREENLAND

ALASKA

ATLANTIC

OCEAN

HUDSON
BAY

GAGNON

CANADA

BANNACK

UNITED STATES

CENTRALIA

RHYOLITE

CALICO

GULF
OF
MEXICO

CARIBBEAN
SEA

PACIFIC

OCEAN

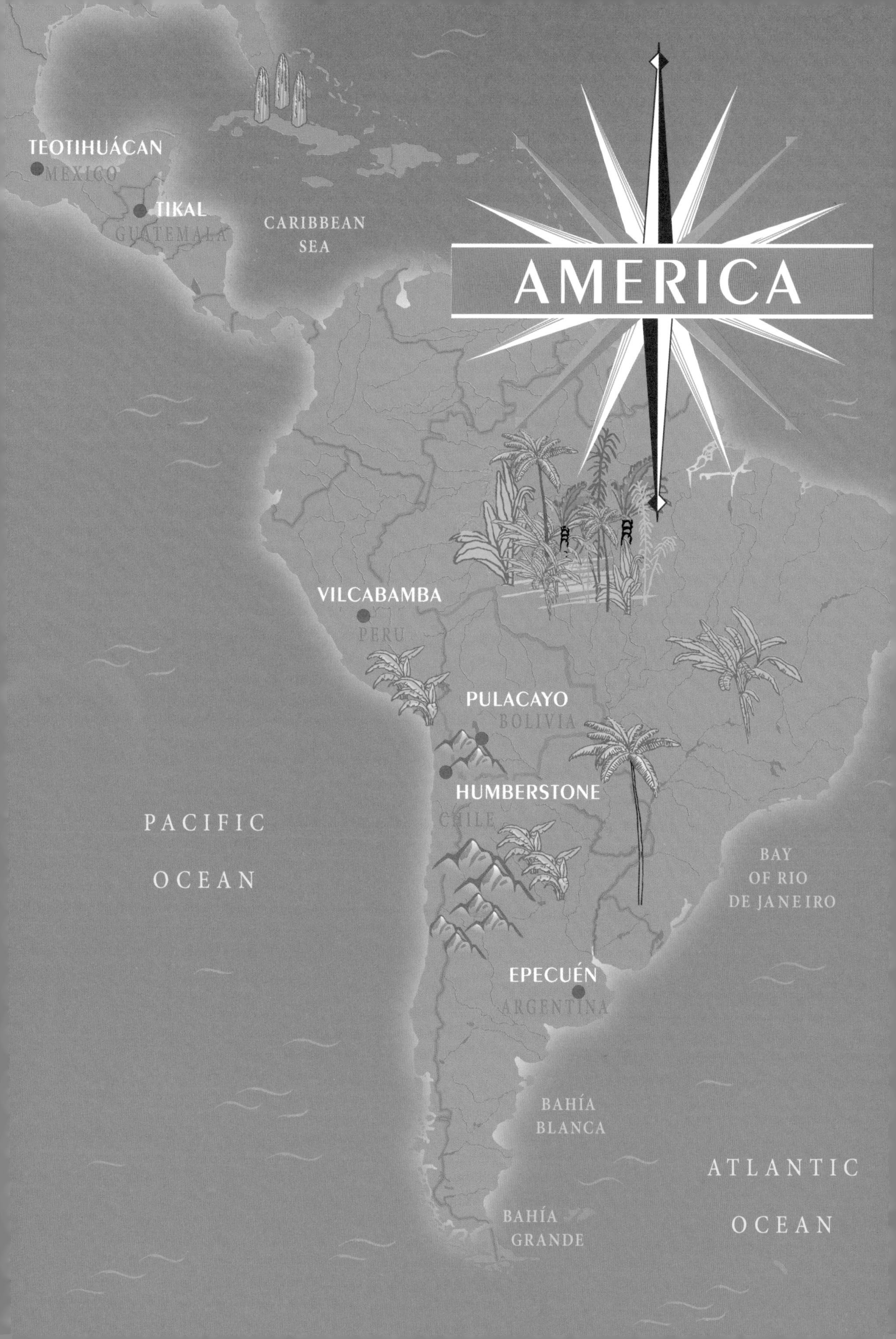

TEOTIHUÁCAN
MEXICO

TIKAL
GUATEMALA

CARIBBEAN
SEA

AMERICA

VILCABAMBA
PERU

PULACAYO
BOLIVIA

HUMBERSTONE
CHILE

PACIFIC

OCEAN

EPECUÉN
ARGENTINA

BAY
OF RIO
DE JANEIRO

BAHÍA
BLANCA

ATLANTIC

OCEAN

BAHÍA
GRANDE

UNITED STATES · 45°09′N, 112°59′W

BANNACK
JUST LIKE A WESTERN

Immortalized in countless Westerns, the great epic of the Far West, an era of conquest and adventure, is relived in the erstwhile capital of Montana every July during the "Bannack Days" festival. At this event enlivened by country music and costumed parades, admirers of John Ford and Clint Eastwood, along with anyone with a penchant for the old days, can experience for themselves the atmosphere of a small town dating from the time of the famous gold rush.

Established at the foot of the Pioneer Mountains in 1862, Bannack owes its existence to the unexpected discovery of a major gold seam that soon attracted not only miners but also hordes of adventurers to the area. Following the expulsion of the Bannock tribe, who had previously inhabited this territory, and after whom the town is named, hotels, shops, blacksmiths, stables, restaurants, and saloons thrived in this settlement that became the capital of Montana in 1864. Sadly, Bannack suffered from a major draw-back: its only resources were those associated with the mine. By the end of the nineteenth century its gold was depleted and production slowed. This triggered the irreversible decline of the town: the industrialists decided to stop working the mine, forcing the inhab-itants to gradually quit Bannack for other towns in Montana, such as Virginia City, which became the new regional capital. During the 1940s the post office, school, stores, and saloons successively closed. The former mining community was transformed into a ghost town before eventually being incorporated into Bannack State Park and embarking upon a new chapter in its history with the arrival of tourists.

Today, countless visitors converge on Bannack in order to admire the sixty or so log houses that remain of the former state capital. A stroll along the streets reveals that the fabric of the buildings has survived the test of time pretty well. Reminders of what a bustling place Bannack once was live on in the form of store-fronts, signage, and painted façades. When the tourists have gone home and the wind whistles through the streets, an Ennio Morricone soundtrack is all that is needed to transport anyone still here back to the heyday of this mining town. One can find oneself imagining that the buildings are not abandoned at all, and that some of the larger-than-life individuals who once called this place home could emerge at any moment: Rose, the keeper of the big saloon, a powerful woman with the hands of a lumberjack and adept at splitting logs with a sure, sharp blow of the ax; beautiful Mary and her fancy man, John Smith, star-crossed lovers who committed suicide in a room at the Grand Hotel in 1908; Henry Plummer, the fearsome sheriff who had no compunction about eliminating anyone who got in the way of his dubious affairs and a murderer to whom twenty-two victims have been attributed. Climbing the creaking staircase that leads up to his office, visitors tremble at the thought that he may turn up at any minute. But instead of ghosts they find wallpaper in tatters, dirty tiles, and worm-eaten doors.

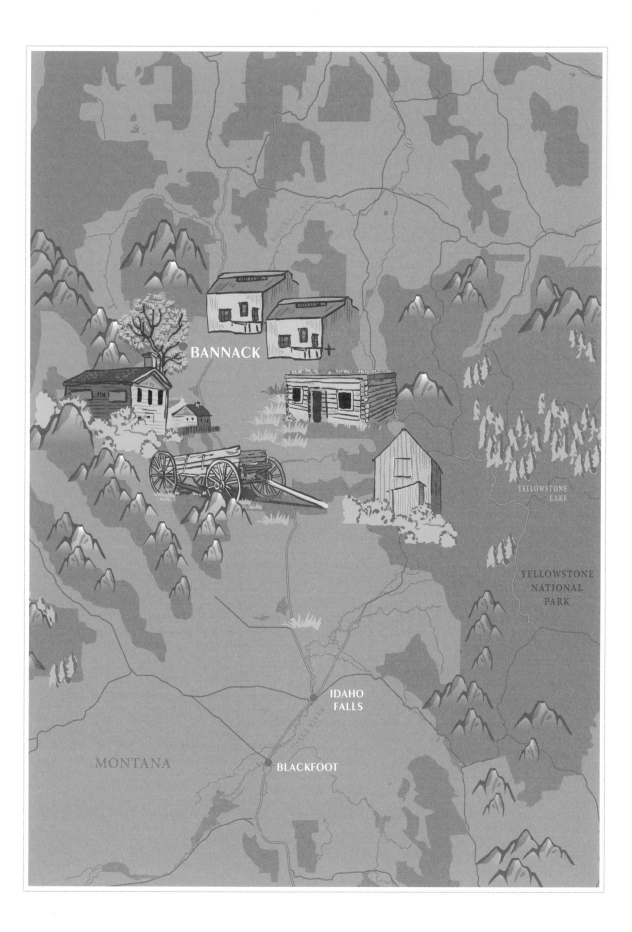

BANNACK

YELLOWSTONE
LAKE

YELLOWSTONE
NATIONAL
PARK

IDAHO
FALLS

MONTANA   BLACKFOOT

UNITED STATES · 34°57′N, 116°52′W

CALICO

FROM GHOST TOWN TO AMUSEMENT PARK

Weatherboard houses roughly lined up along a dirt road; rickety façades decorated with signs; sidewalks alternating with broad wooden galleries in front of which it is easy to imagine horses tied up and awaiting their owners: the look of Calico is virtually identical to that of the Lucky Luke comics and John Wayne films, a reminder of all those towns that emerged as some kind of would-be El Dorado only to disappear a few years later, abandoned as quickly as they had sprung into life. At this place located two hundred kilometers from the California coast, where a narrow canyon emerges into the desert, the gold rush was actually a silver rush. The first seam of silver ore was discovered here in 1881. Within six years, Calico had 1,200 inhabitants and five hundred working mines. It became prosperous and before long offered all the facilities required by its population of prospectors: hotels, stores, chapels, a newspaper (the *Calico Print*), not to mention twenty-two saloons and almost as many whorehouses. When the price of silver plummeted in 1890, the pioneers immediately packed up and left. No matter: in less than ten years they had earned at least $86 million!

After a short respite during which the town managed to get by on the extraction of borax, a salt used in photography and in the manufacture of fertilizer and soap, Calico was finally abandoned in 1907. Around the same time, further borax deposits were discovered farther north.

There was never any plan to turn Calico into a ghost town. In the end it was reborn thanks to a very different kind of activity. In the 1920s Walter Knott, a farmer from the Los Angeles area, had considerable success selling boysenberries, a hybrid of the blackberry and the raspberry, from a roadside stand. After a while the farmer opened a restaurant in which his wife served the—by then famous—little fruits as a specialty. In order to entertain customers waiting in line, he had the ingenious idea of giving his restaurant a Wild West setting. He therefore surrounded it with buildings removed from various ghost towns in the vicinity, including many elements brought from Calico.

By the 1950s this new venture, Knott's Berry Farm, which still belongs to the family today, was highly successful and went on to develop into a bona fide amusement park—inspiring a certain Walt Disney to create his own! In the midst of the attractions was the ghost town built by the farmer, centered

Calico has been designated the "official ghost town of the Silver Rush"

CALIFORNIA

LANCASTER

CALICO

VICTORVILLE

SAN GABRIEL
MOUNTAINS

LOS ANGELES

SALTON
SEA

PACIFIC

OCEAN

ESCONDIDO

around Calico Square and a saloon. The plan to restore the real Calico, where no more than half a dozen of the original buildings remained standing, was also the Knotts' idea. Starting in 1951, based on old photographs, the family rebuilt Calico exactly as it was, including the saloon, the sheriff's office, the general stores, the neat and tidy school resembling something out of *Little House on the Prairie*, and the fire station, complete with bell and an authentic horse-drawn water pump. Shrewd entrepreneurs that they were, the Knotts added a number of restaurants and souvenir shops, and also replicated various attractions from Knott's Berry Farm: a house built of glass bottles (inspired by another ghost town, Rhyolite in Nevada), and the Mystery Shack, filled with optical illusions such as water that flows uphill and distorting mirrors. The Knotts also replaced the original "iron horse" with a replica. The five hundred meter railroad circuit takes visitors into the mountain-side, where they are taken on a tour of a silver mine. The setting has been recreated with great attention to detail. Here and there, ancient wagons and plaster cowboys accentuate the picturesque character of the place, while brawls and gun-fights are enacted at set times. Finally, Calico is brought to the attention of drivers down below on the Los Angeles–Las Vegas freeway by an enormous sign in giant letters emblazoned on the mountainside.

In 2005, despite its commercial trappings, the governor of California declared Calico the "official ghost town of the Silver Rush" in view of the fact that it was one of the most authentic locations dating from this heroic period. Visitors to the town are occasionally irritated by its "amusement park" character. Those in the know simply pass through on their way deeper into the mountains, to the heart of the remote canyons which, for their part, have barely changed since the great days of the Wild West.

The look of Calico is virtually identical to that of the Lucky Luke comics and John Wayne films

CALICO
THE GOLD RUSH

In addition to the incentive of striking it rich, the sharp increase in the nineteenth century in the number of towns like Calico, which owe their existence to deposits of gold, silver, or some other precious metal, was stimulated by advances in the fields of transportation and communication. Whether in North America, Africa, or Australia, the scenario was always the same: as soon as a deposit was discovered, news would spread like wildfire and migrants would flood in by ship or by railroad, the invention of the century. Towns equipped with all the infrastructure required for community life then sprang up within a matter of months, frequently under harsh conditions. Often located in regions that were difficult to reach, the living conditions in towns like this were extremely precarious for the miners and their families. As soon as a deposit was exhausted, the town that had developed around it would disappear—just as anarchically as it had sprung into being. And while the lucky few made their fortunes, most prospectors returned to their place of origin barely any wealthier than when they had set out.

UNITED STATES · 40°48´N, 76°20´W

CENTRALIA
THE EARTH FOREVER SCORCHED

A fire that has been impossible to extinguish since it started…more than fifty years ago! Centralia has been living with this incredible perpetual blaze since May 1962.

In preparation for Memorial Day, when Americans who gave their lives for their country are remembered, a group of municipal workers set fire to a pile of garbage next to one of the cemeteries of this small town in Pennsylvania. No one noticed the fire spread into the underground coal mine whose galleries extend beneath the town, and this act of either carelessness or stupidity was to seal Centralia's fate. The elderly folk hereabouts tell how the catastrophe was predicted almost a century before it occurred. One Sunday at the end of the nineteenth century, a local priest, incensed at the bad ways of his parishioners, is said to have prophesied that their entire town—with the exception of his church and its cemetery—would be engulfed in flame. Apparently his anger did not go unheeded, for all that remains of Centralia today is a church, four cemeteries, and a municipal building in which a fire engine is kept, just in case…

In this working-class town founded in 1866, following the discovery of a coal seam, everything

It was the story of Centralia that inspired the creators of the video game Silent Hill

was organized around its mine. Centralia possessed neither grand monuments nor spectacular facilities, but instead rows of small houses along the two main streets, two churches, a few stores, a railroad station, a baseball field, schools, and various public buildings. It was a small town like countless others in the United States, a town not overendowed with character, but nevertheless a place where generations of working people, immigrants predominantly from Ireland, Poland, and Ukraine, lived peaceably alongside one another.

Despite the harsh realities of a life spent extracting coal, there was a strong sense of solidarity in this mining community, at least until the disaster that initiated the exodus. Although the underground fire went unnoticed at first, over the following months it was responsible for a number of truly disturbing incidents. The fire could not be put out, and it slowly spread, releasing jets of carbon monoxide into the atmosphere through large fissures in the ground and producing plumes of smoke that seemed to be issuing from hell itself. Worried by the nauseating odors emanating from the underground blaze, many residents left town. Due to the lack of alternative opportunities, however, many others

stayed behind, coping as best they could. In 1981 a boy had a narrow escape when the ground beneath him subsided, almost swallowing him up. This prompted local and federal authorities to evacuate the town, which still numbered a thousand or so residents. As people left, their houses were pulled down, and the notorious Catholic church at the heart of the sinister prophecy suffered the same fate. In 2002 the town's zip code was withdrawn.

Since then, a number of diehards have clung on, shutting themselves away from the prying eyes of tourists and refusing to consign Centralia to the realm of memory. Centralia has become a Pennsylvania attraction. It has also inspired the creators of the *Silent Hill* video game, which has now been adapted for the cinema. It is not difficult to imagine how this place could inspire any movie directors who happen to find themselves on the somewhat surreal Route 42. Once lined with bars and stores but now deserted, this is the starting point of a network of tarred roads that now lead nowhere. Emerging here and there from the vegetation along these roads are piles of—in some cases warm—stones, the remains of the demolished houses. In the vicinity of the cemetery, the only place that still seems almost spick-and-span, with US flags marking its graves, the ground continues to smoke. No one has ever succeeded in extinguishing the fire, which is buckling the asphalt and causing fissures to open up. To the sides of these crevasses clings moss, as if in defiance of this project of ruination. Experts believe the fire could continue to burn for at least another two hundred years, the time it would take to consume all the underground coal.

The only people who visit this desolate town nowadays are tourists—apart from a handful of former residents, some of them traveling from far away, who gather on the hill on which the Orthodox church of St. Ignatius still stands, the only place in Centralia that is still alive. When the bells ring to announce the church service, they spend a brief moment remembering the happy days before the place they once called home was devoured by an infernal blaze.

No one has ever succeeded in extinguishing the fire, which is buckling the asphalt and causing crevasses to open up in the ground

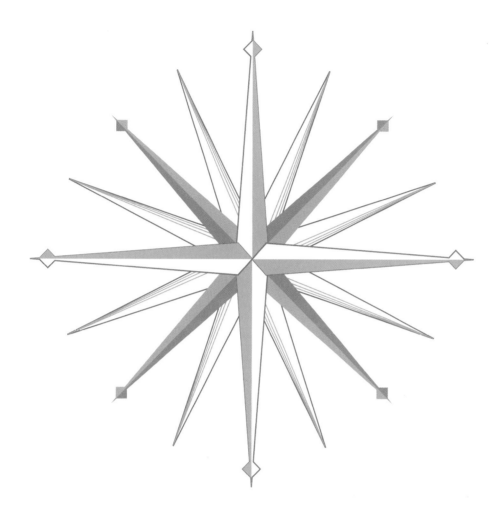

The fire could continue to burn
for at least another
two hundred years,
the time it would take to consume
all the underground coal

ARGENTINA · 37°08′S, 62°48′W

EPECUÉN

THE CORROSIVE POWER OF SALT

In 1985 the lakeside resort of Epecuén boasted some 250 hotels and fitness/health centers and almost as many cafés, restaurants, and businesses of every kind. The purpose of all this infrastructure was to cater to the needs of the twenty-five thousand or so mainly Argentinian tourists who flocked to the renowned spa, located southwest of Buenos Aires, each season. It has to be said that this neat and tidy resort town, which grew up in the 1920s, possessed a significant asset: it was built on the shores of a warm-water lake reputed to be rich in minerals and possessing one of the highest levels of salinity in the world. The first vacationers would start to arrive at the railroad station each spring. Most of the visitors had come to take the waters and were impatient to immerse themselves in Lake Epecuén, where, as in the Dead Sea, bathers could float without even trying. The bay lined with beaches, on which shade was provided by straw umbrellas, was demarcated by an enormous levee describing an arc. Footbaths and hotel pools all over the town were also filled with the "miraculous" water for which great claims were made—not to mention the magnificent municipal baths equipped with a diving board, bar, and solarium. Alongside the soccer stadium, a large square with swings provided entertainment for children. The roads were jammed with cars and the sidewalks filled with young women in skimpy dresses. And all beneath an azure sky. It is difficult to imagine, during this blissful time, that a natural drama was quietly unfolding that would wipe Villa Lago Epecuén off the map.

This neat and tidy resort town possessed a significant asset: it was built on the shores of a warm-water lake rich in minerals

In 1975, in order to regulate the flow of water between the different lakes in the region, the provincial government built a canal, along with a network of sluice gates, linking several of the lakes. The system was designed to avoid both droughts and flooding. After 1976, the year of the coup d'état that brought General Jorge Rafael Videla to power, maintenance of the system ceased, and in the general disorder of those years of bloody repression, no one was appointed to oversee the sluices, barriers, and lagoons. However, what was originally intended as a solution developed into a problem: as a result of a connecting vessel effect, the water level of Lake Epecuén rose by fifty centimeters per year, threatening the buildings

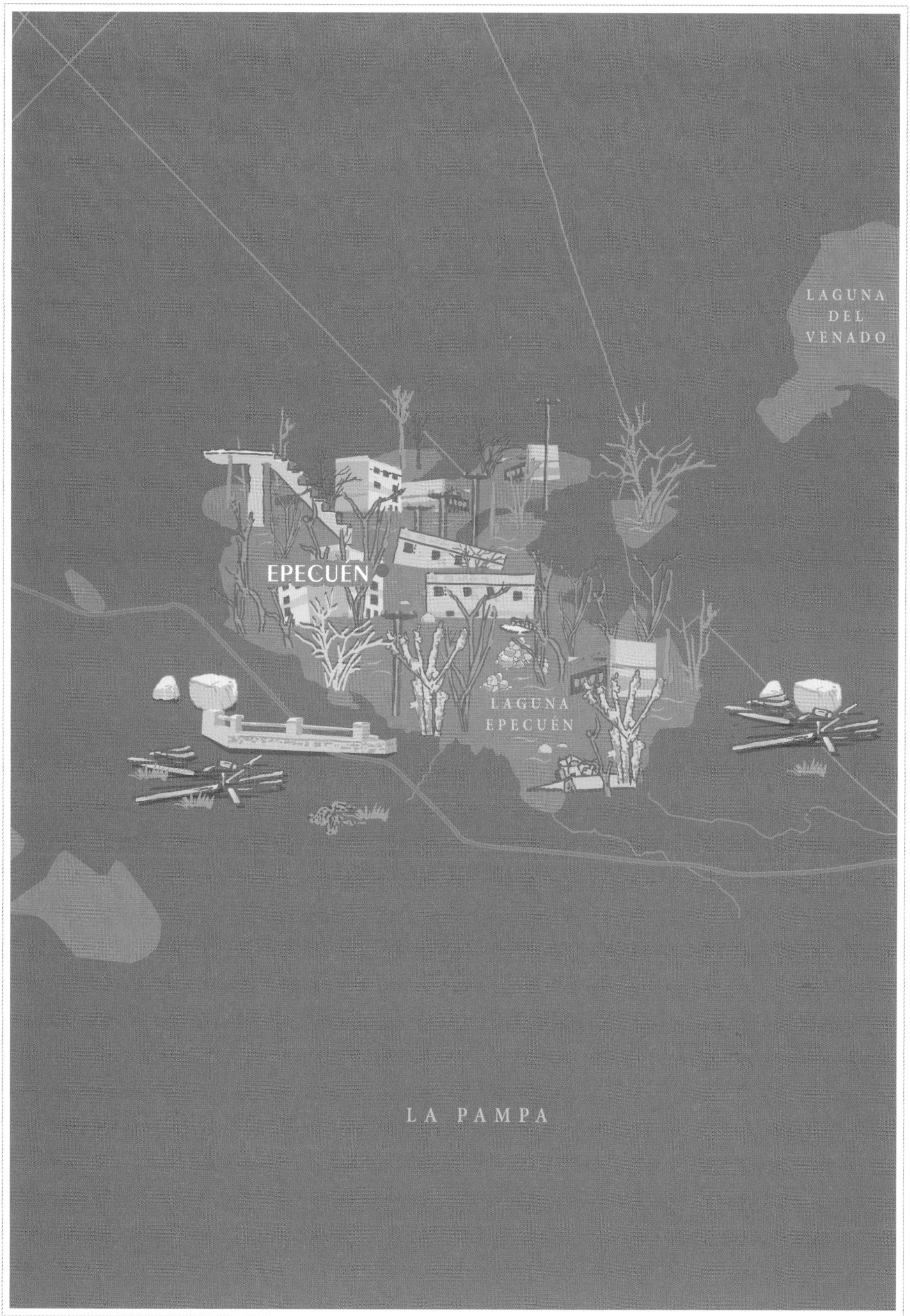

LAGUNA
DEL
VENADO

EPECUÉN

LAGUNA
EPECUÉN

LA PAMPA

In 2008, when the water
eventually subsided,
Epecuén reappeared.
The scenes were apocalyptic.
What emerged from
the blue waters of the lake
were wrecked buildings,
dead trees, and gaunt, ghostly
electricity poles bleached
white by the salt

on its shores. The local people reinforced the enormous levee, whose curved shape can still be made out on satellite photos today. At daybreak on November 10, 1985, the levee was lashed by waves whipped up by the violent *sudesta* winds and exacerbated by particularly heavy rainfall. It gave way, with catastrophic results. The water, highly corrosive due to its high salt content, flooded into the streets, sweeping away cars, invading hotels and the soccer stadium, and driving people from their homes. The population responded by moving objects up to higher floors or transporting them to safety via the trucks and tractors that shuttled continuously between Epecuén and the town of Carhué a few kilometers away. After two weeks the resort stood under two meters of water. Within the space of a few months, the water level had risen to ten meters, and the roof of the Grand Hotel disappeared beneath the surface. While cement proved resistant, metallic items rapidly oxidized and silently, beneath the water, structures gave way. Anything made of metal was transformed into powder.

In 2008, when the water eventually subsided, Epecuén reappeared. The scenes were apocalyptic. What emerged from the blue waters of the lake were wrecked buildings, dead trees, and gaunt, ghostly

electricity poles bleached white by the salt—the aftermath, one might have imagined, of a bombardment or earthquake. Epecuén was finished, and with it the pleasures of strolling on a summer's evening to the Confitería Coradini, which was open all year round and a delightful place to enjoy a delicious cup of hot chocolate in winter too, or to Hotel Altieri, of which nothing remained but a section of wall and a staircase leading nowhere.

EPECUÉN
A MEMORY ERASED

Towns disappear beneath the water for different reasons. Whereas Epecuén's fate was the result of a natural catastrophe (although human negligence clearly played a part), other places, such as Shi Cheng in China or Tignes in the high-lying Isère Valley in France, were sacrificed in execution of an official decision or for the sake of economic interests. What does a corporation like EDF, which started work on the construction of an enormous concrete dam at Tignes in 1950, care about the memory of a particular place? After confronting the objections of the locals regarding the local economy and the environment, the French energy concern submerged the ancient stone houses beneath the waters of an artificial lake. For a number of decades the remains of these buildings reappeared at regular intervals during the inspection of the dam. Now, the checking is carried out by underwater robots, and so it is no longer necessary to completely empty the lake. The flooded town can rest easy: its former inhabitants will no longer be coming back to relive their memories. Old Tignes has gone forever.

CANADA · 62°00′N, 110°30′W

GAGNON

WIPED OFF THE MAP BY A VOTE

The only thing that keeps alive the memory of this town cut down in its prime is a Facebook page on which registered users can post their photos and documents. Gagnon's fate could be described as surreal: it was quite simply wiped off the face of the earth by a vote of the National Assembly in Quebec in October 1984. A few months later, all that was left behind after the bulldozers and mechanical diggers had finished was a vast expanse of freshly turned earth and the two roads whose junction once marked the center of town. One can well imagine how awful this must have been for the town's four thousand or so inhabitants, many of whom had played a part in its heroic beginnings.

The town owed its name to Onésime Gagnon, a former lieutenant governor of the province of Quebec who, in addition to his various other ministerial duties, was minister of mines. It was only natural that the town that grew up following the discovery of iron ore deposits near the Jeannine and Barbel lakes in the Côte-Nord region of Quebec should be named after him. The community was incorporated in 1960. Its inhabitants—Québécois born and bred as well as immigrants from Portugal and Italy—were happy to live in the modern and well-equipped town despite the difficult climatic conditions and its relative isolation. Pending construction of a road linking the town to Baie-Comeau, which would not be completed until 1987—in other words, three years after the official dissolution of the community—Gagnon was accessible only by plane or train. In this working-class community, whose residents saw themselves as colonists at the end of the world, solidarity was more than just a word and the local social life, which centered on the lake, was lively. In winter there were hockey and skating; in summer, water sports. In the 1970s, not long after the founding of the town, things started to get difficult as the deposits gradually dwindled. In 1977 the mine closed and production shifted to Fire Lake, ninety kilometers northwest of Gagnon. The workers played the game and put up with the exhausting traveling as best they could. The ax finally fell in 1984 when Fire Lake mine was, in turn, closed. The residents of Gagnon were informed that their town would soon disappear from the map and that they would be paid compensation for the loss of their homes.

Today, all that remains of the town are a few opencast mines. Nothing is left of the houses, typical examples of 1960s architecture, other than a number of moving testimonies left by nostalgic visitors, for example, a sign written in blue ink that has already started to fade: "We lived in this town for twenty happy years. We will never ever forget you Gagnon, the place of our youth and long-lost dreams." In 2015 the former inhabitants of the town, a group of people decidedly more consistent in their outlook than the administrative decision makers, are planning to get together for a day to remember the old times.

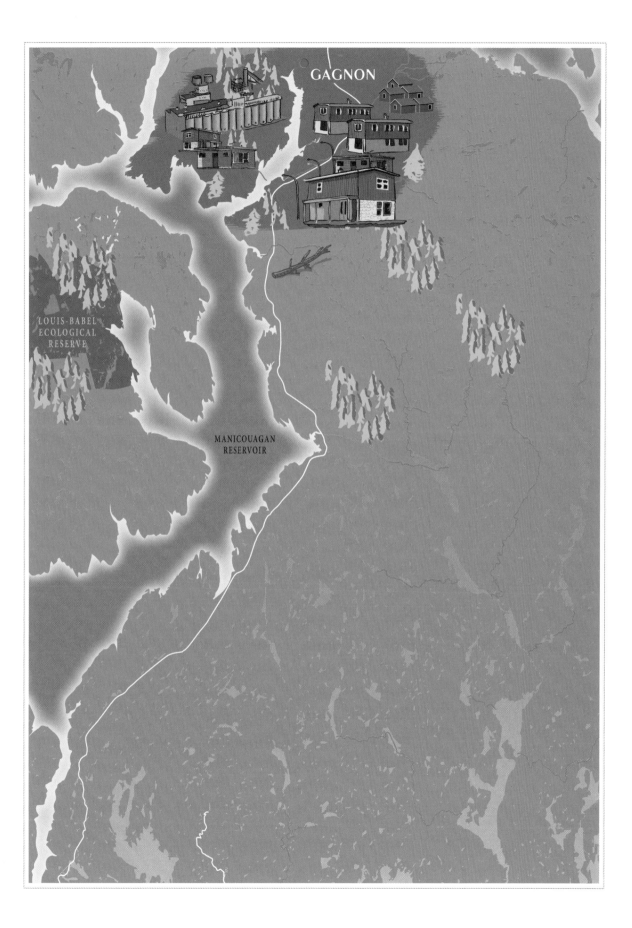

GAGNON

LOUIS-BABEL
ECOLOGICAL
RESERVE

MANICOUAGAN
RESERVOIR

CHILE · 20°12′S, 69°48′W

HUMBERSTONE
"WE ARE SORROW"

This is the driest region on earth, a place where records fall like flies. In the Atacama Desert the temperature can fluctuate by as much as 50 degrees Fahrenheit in a single day, and the ultraviolet rays are so powerful that it is essential to wear sunglasses and cover any exposed skin with sunblock. In some areas it has not rained for four hundred years—and yet a town was established in this inhospitable environment. Humberstone owes its existence to the presence below ground of an extremely precious mineral used in the manufacture of gunpowder. In 1872 Thomas Humberstone, a British engineer, discovered the deposit while exploring the coast of Chile and went on to found the Peru Nitrate Company. More than two hundred extraction sites, all English and interconnected via a railroad network, were opened up. This was followed by the construction of various factories for the processing of the mineral and the establishment of a number of mining towns. Initially of modest size, Humberstone developed rapidly with the arrival of the railroad at the end of the nineteenth century. Along with Chilean, Bolivian, and Peruvian miners, the trains also brought adventurers and fortune seekers from all over the world to Humberstone. Although the 1929 slump and the invention in Germany of synthetic nitrates dampened the output of the factory towns, 1934 marked the high point in Humberstone's fortunes. Then boasting 3,700 inhabitants, it was bought that year by a Chilean corporation. Its enormous theater attracted artists from all over the world, its *pulpería* (general store) was the best stocked in the whole of Chile, and its enormous swimming pool, constructed out of the hull of a wrecked ship, was talked about far and wide. Nevertheless, in the 1940s the Chilean saltpeter industry gradually died. Humberstone was definitively abandoned in February 1960 after eighty years of mining activity. It could have become just another ghost town in the history of mining, but it was not to be. Europeans and native South Americans worked together in this hostile environment to create a unique identity, the *cultura pampina*, with its own way of talking, its own dress code, and its own values closely bound up with saltpeter. This culture is celebrated each year during the *fiesta pampina* or saltpeter week, when the descendants of the original inhabitants converge on the former mining town. The deserted streets are brought to life, men in traditional costume perform a dance that involves the brandishing of handkerchiefs, others play a form of bowls, and all reminisce about the community spirit of the olden days, when the dry air was filled with the noise of mechanical diggers. This highly specific culture even has its own hymn, "Yo Soy Pampino," whose words are filled with nostalgia for what is no more: "The saltpeter works have closed, they exist only in my heart. We were the future, we were splendor. Now we are neglect, we are sorrow…"

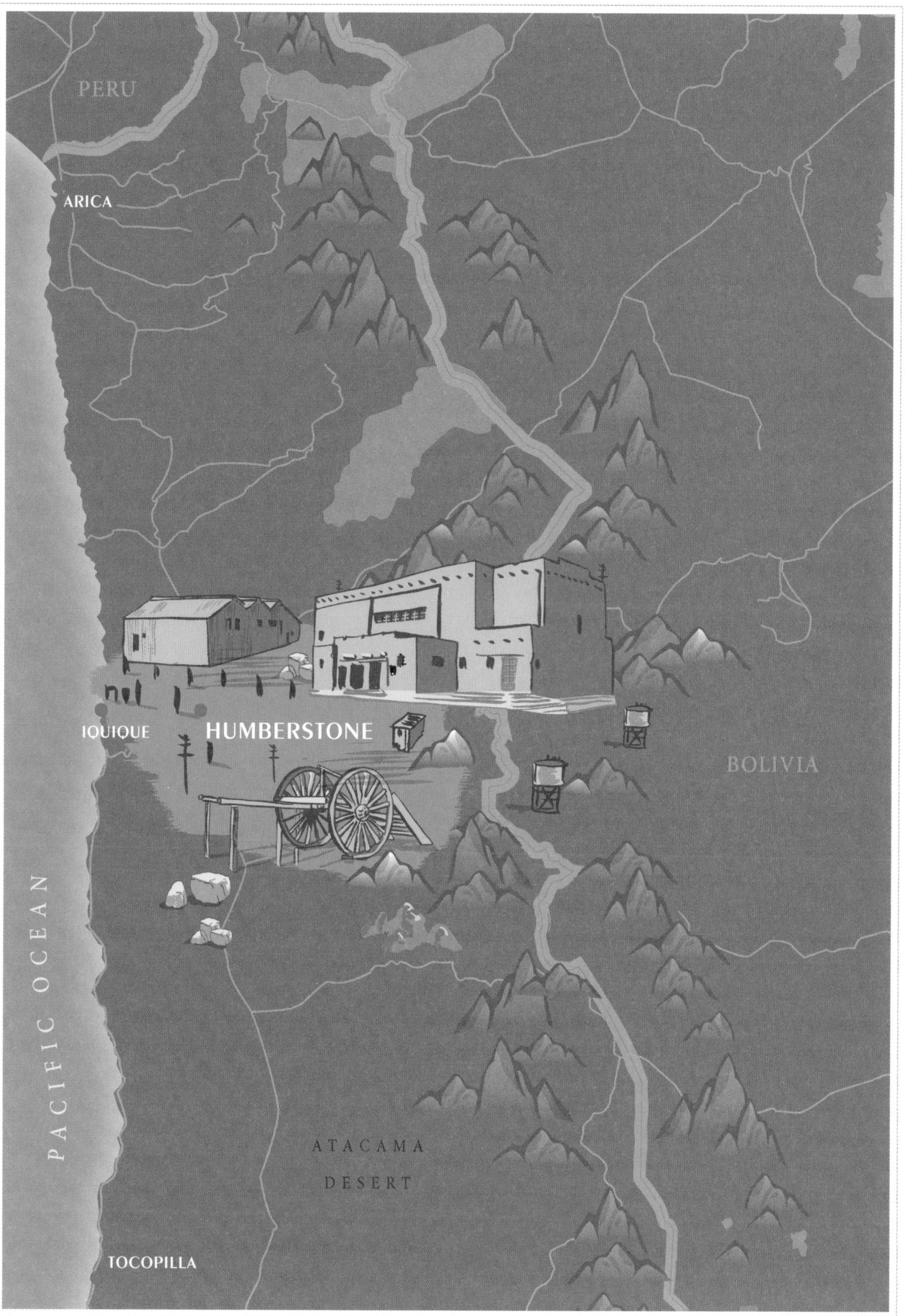
PERU
ARICA
IQUIQUE
HUMBERSTONE
BOLIVIA
PACIFIC OCEAN
ATACAMA
DESERT
TOCOPILLA

BOLIVIA · 20°23´S, 66°42´W

PULACAYO
REVOLUTIONARY CITY

Once upon a time a man was riding a mule through the Bolivian mountains when his mount fell, sending him tumbling into a shallow ravine. There, on the ground next to him, he discovered a good-sized nugget of silver, which he took to the neighboring village to be valued. "Where did you find it?" he was asked. Not wishing to reveal the precise spot, the man replied, "*Donde mula cayó*" (Where my mule fell). Corrupted over the course of the years, these words were to become the name of this mining town, which, in the nineteenth century, possessed the largest silver deposits in Bolivia. Located on a mountainside in the midst of a dusty, stony landscape, Pulacayo's other claim to fame is that it was the first mining town in the country to be served by the railroad, thereby attracting hordes of miners looking for work as well as traders and adventurers seeking their fortunes. Tradition has it that one of these trains, transporting the precious metal to the Pacific coast, was attacked by the renowned Butch Cassidy.

By the beginning of the twentieth century, the town boasted more than twenty thousand inhabitants, including seven thousand miners and, as a major commercial center and capital of the country's mining industry, it became Bolivia's second city. Its prosperity was evident from its *pulpería*, or general store, where the wealthiest residents could pamper their refined tastes with French wines, Italian shoes, English fabrics, and Argentinian meat. Moreover, photographs of the day show the miners dressed in European style. Pulacayo had its own newspaper (the *Presencia*), a theater, numerous social clubs, and even a brothel, where many a bachelor miner ended up. Within workers' circles, however, there was discussion, there was indignation, and there was plotting, for the train had also brought communist ideas to the town. During the 1940s a number of strikes and attempts to form unions were bloodily repressed. In addition to the harsh realities of the mine, glaring social injustices were reflected in the town planning. Barbed wire separated the prosperous districts from those assigned to the poor, with the immensely wealthy on one side and miners working in appalling conditions on the other. The pride of the town, the famous *Pulacayo Thesis*, signed by miners and representatives of the union movements at the foot of the mine in 1946 following the unrest, is today considered an extremely important document in union history. Having been nationalized in 1952, the mine eventually began to dry up, and membership of the mining cooperative that had been established in 1962 slowly dwindled. The golden age of Pulacayo was well and truly over.

Today the ghost town still numbers a few hundred residents, who raise llamas, scratch out a living through bartering, and occasionally open their humble homes to serve traditional *mate de coca* to visitors. The eldest of them are fond of telling stories about how life once was in Pulacayo, when the streets were bustling with life and before steam locomotives had become museum pieces—memories of a lost paradise that above all was the scene of their youth.

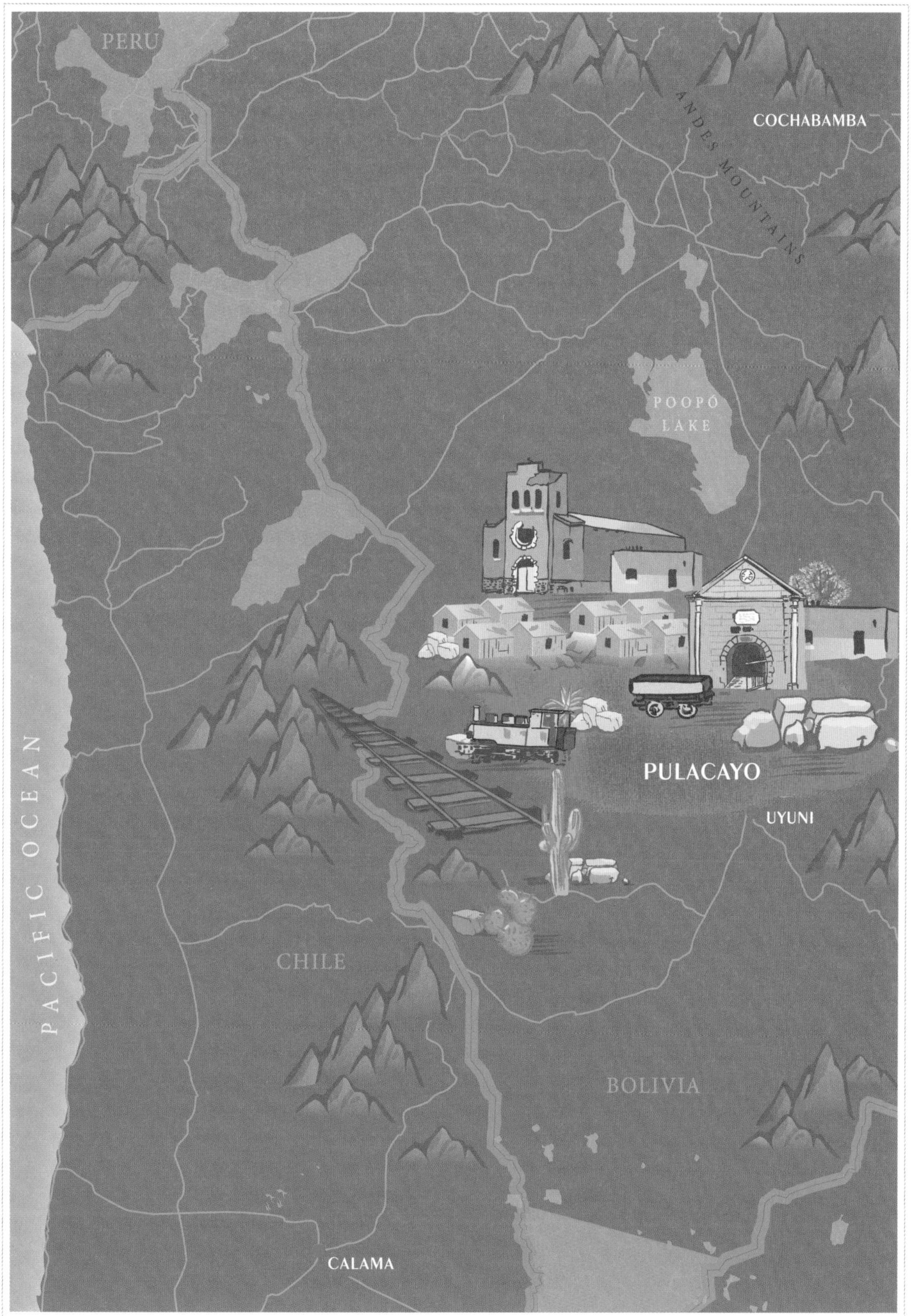
PERU
ANDES MOUNTAINS
COCHABAMBA
POOPÓ LAKE
PACIFIC OCEAN
PULACAYO
UYUNI
CHILE
BOLIVIA
CALAMA

UNITED STATES · 36°54′N, 116°49′W

RHYOLITE
A SHOOTING STAR

It survived for only five short years, between 1904 and 1908. Located in the Nevada desert, some two hours by road from Las Vegas, this town was nevertheless born under the most favorable auspices, thanks to the enthusiasm of a community of proprietor-miners attracted by the quantity of gold below ground. Nature, however, had other plans.

If the remains of the town are substantial compared to its brief lifespan, this is because Rhyolite, unlike the majority of mining towns in the American West, was built largely of stone. As early as 1905, it possessed all the infrastructure essential to the life of a substantial town: drinking water, electricity, a town hall, a school, a hospital, hotels, stores, a considerable number of saloons, and last but not least a prison, which would come into its own when criminal activity rose in proportion to the decline in mining activity. As far as leisure activities were concerned, the "Chicago of the West," as it was nicknamed at the time, boasted a swimming pool, an opera house, a theater, and—to the great delight of the gold hunters, who wasted no time in paying court to the actresses who came in by train—no fewer than three variety halls.

In 1908, the optimism of the town's ten thousand inhabitants was swept away by rumor. People began to claim that the size of the gold deposits had been overestimated by the founders of the city. A miner was said to have emerged from his mine empty-handed one day, exclaiming: "There's no more gold!" This destroyed the confidence of the residents in their gold seam. Convinced that the high concentration of the precious metal in the ground was a mere fabrication, and furious with the bankers who no longer supported their investment in tools and machinery, the youngest miners quit Rhyolite more or less on the spot, with those more advanced in years and their families hard on their heels. Following this initial wave of departures, things went from bad to worse. Actresses stopped coming to the town and the theaters and casinos closed, provoking an economic crisis that resulted in the storekeepers closing up shop. In spring 1908 the town was forced to switch off its municipal lighting, signaling the end of Rhyolite.

It is now known that the rumors were unfounded: there was still gold in the ground at Rhyolite. It is also known that the San Francisco earthquake of 1906 and the stock exchange panic of 1907 caused the bankers' ambitious investments in the town to dry up, and without investment Rhyolite was doomed. These days the former mining town is on the Death Valley tourist trail. In visiting these stone ruins, sightseers are able to discover one of the key locations in which the rush for gold, and with it a new life, was played out.

NEVADA

DEATH
VALLEY

RHYOLITE

LAS
VEGAS

SAN GABRIEL
MOUNTAINS

LOS ANGELES

MEXICO · 19°41′N, 98°52′W

TEOTIHUACÁN

BETWEEN THE SUN AND THE MOON

Attracting 1.6 million visitors a year and boasting six hundred pyramids and two thousand monuments scattered over some eighty-two square kilometers, Teotihuacán, listed in 1987 as a UNESCO World Heritage Site, is an archaeological megalopolis on an even greater scale than ancient Rome. Located fifty kilometers northeast of Mexico City, Teotihuacán, once one of the most important cities in Mesoamerica, is now an enormous archaeology park surrounded by suburbs of modern modest dwellings. However, these houses in no way detract from the sense of awe experienced by visitors at the extraordinary panorama that greets them at the top of the Pyramid of the Sun. Laid out before their eyes is a plateau some 2,300 meters above sea level that extends all the way to the distant mountains scalloping the horizon. The only elevations on this plateau are the city's pyramids and temples.

Teotihuacán reached its apogee in the fifth century A.D., when its influence spread far and wide

Of all pre-Columbian sites, Teotihuacán has been the most studied, measured, written about, and classified, and yet virtually nothing is known about its origins—not the ethnicity of the people who built it, the language spoken in the city, or even what it was originally called! The name Teotihuacán, meaning "city of the gods," was attributed to the city by a later people, the Mexicas, long after its decline.

Until the 1940s, archaeologists believed the city to have been founded by the Toltec people, who were contemporaneous with the Maya. This thesis was subsequently rejected as the Toltec did not possess the necessary cultural sophistication at the time the city was built (around 300 B.C.). More recently, various authors have suggested that it was founded by the Totonac, a peace-loving people from the Veracruz region who have survived to the present day. The most likely explanation is that the enormous city was established over the course of several centuries by ethnic groups all influenced to some degree by the Olmec culture that laid the foundations for the main Mesoamerican empires. How is it that a small agricultural colony was able to become the capital of the region? Gaining importance a few dozen years before Christ and eventually developing into an apparently anarchic but in fact highly organized (at least on the evidence of its rational urban planning concept) melting pot, Teotihuacán reached its apogee in the fifth century A.D., an era in which the influence of its cultural, social, and religious model

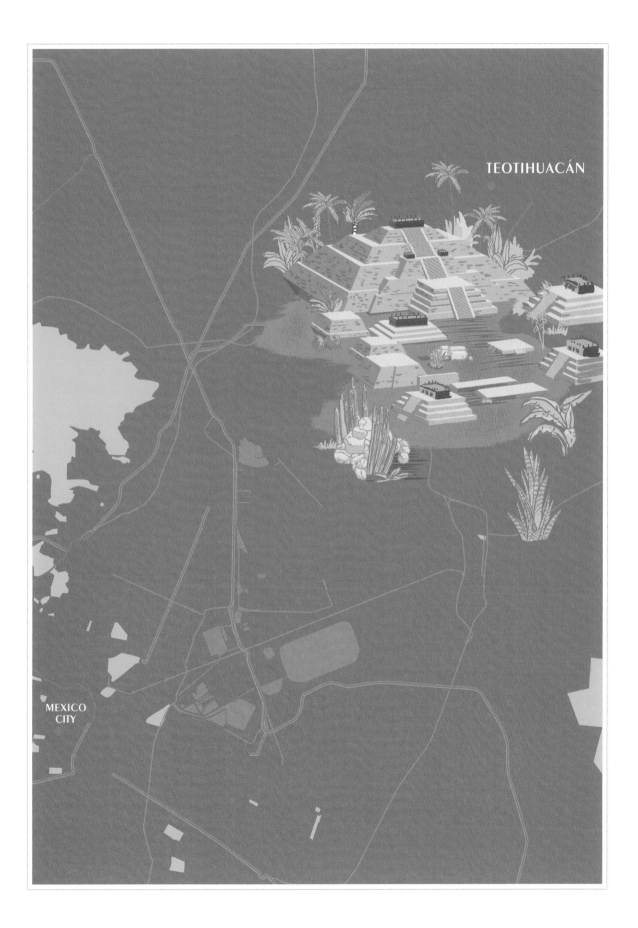

TEOTIHUACÁN

MEXICO
CITY

reached far and wide. At this time the city was, it seems, the most powerful and populous on the American continent (with a population estimated variously at between fifty and two hundred thousand). Its downfall, for reasons still not fully understood, occurred between the seventh and eighth centuries. Teotihuacán may well have been ransacked: the religious complex known as the Citadel was certainly demolished, burned, and crushed, and its remnants scattered over a distance of several kilometers, as if the perpetrators wanted to rule out any renaissance by pulverizing the symbol of the city. The emergence of other cultural centers around A.D. 700 accelerated the exodus from the city, and the ruins of this vast urban project were abandoned to slow erosion by the Mexican winds.

Because of its dimensions and prestige, however, Teotihuacán was not completely neglected. The Aztec people, who founded Mexico in the fourteenth century, made it the destination of regular ritual pilgrimages and the Spanish conquistadors were awestruck by the ruins. The first excavations were undertaken in 1675, and over the course of the centuries Teotihuacán was to become famous all over the world. Quite apart from its gigantic scale, the site is simply unique. This urban space, whose geometric lines appear very modern, speaks of a

Each year Teotihuacán

is visited by

1.6 million tourists

from all over the world

deeply mystifying civilization utterly in thrall to an implacable religion. The city-state, whose political power was held by the priests, was conceived as a symbolic representation of the universe and a place of communication with the gods. The ground plan seems to have been based on the course of the sun and oriented toward a particular mountain. One of the main axes leads from the Pyramid of the Moon (containing the skeletons of human sacrificial victims dating from different stages in its construction), past the Pyramid of the Sun (an enormous structure some sixty-five meters high), to the eastern side of the Citadel. This complex contains the Temple of the Feathered Serpent, also known as the Temple of Quetzalcóatl.

Constructed around A.D. 150, this temple is surrounded by a square precinct. Its tiers are decorated with the heads of serpents once painted in bright colors, each weighing no less than four metric tons. Beneath the temple lie the remains of numbers of young people sacrificed in order to appease the bloodthirsty gods. Although many years have passed since these particular gods lost their power, here their memory lives on. All the more so as only a small fraction of the archaeological zone has yet been excavated.

Teotihuacán is an archaeological megalopolis with six hundred pyramids and two thousand monuments scattered over some eighty-two square kilometers

GUATEMALA · 17°13′N, 89°36′W

TIKAL
FLEEING FAMINE

The entrances to the main clusters of ruins at Tikal are no more than a few hundred meters apart, but to cross this distance by foot is almost like passing from the status of tourist to that of explorer, so dense is the vegetation. At least the walk prepares visitors for the visual shock that awaits them in the Great Plaza, for here, soaring into the air in front of them, are the two most remarkable pyramids of this extraordinary city that was the cradle of the Maya civilization (A.D. 250–900). Massive and mysterious, the two structures face each other squarely, their summits reached via steep staircases cut into each of their four sides. From the tops, claim certain archaeologists, priests once communicated from one temple to another. Can it be mere chance that one of the translations of the word *Tikal* is "the place of voices"?

The site consists of far more than its main acropolises, however. At the heart of what is now a national park, it comprises a whole collection of wonders: temples, royal palaces, and monumental sculptures over which the twin pyramids seem to watch from their fifty-meter elevation. Many of the edifices are clad in bas-reliefs, some badly eroded, whose symbolism is understood by only the most learned of visitors, and the entire site is dotted with steles inscribed with hieroglyphic texts telling the story of what was once one of the most powerful of Mayan capitals. During its heyday, around A.D. 600, the city is thought to have numbered some five hundred thousand inhabitants. Hieroglyphic writing, the arts, astronomy, and architecture were taught here, attracting artists, intellectuals, and aristocratic families

from all over the region. Within two hundred years, the jungle had completely smothered the ruins. How was it possible for centuries of civilization to be erased so rapidly? Some people believe that Tikal was not destroyed but abandoned, probably due to some climatic problem that depleted local resources. It is known that the Maya territory was affected by a long drought at the end of the eighth century. One thing is certain: the city was abandoned for good in the tenth. Thanks to oral tradition, however, its memory never died, facilitating its rediscovery at the end of the seventeenth century. The first official exploration of Tikal was undertaken in 1848, a time when the city could be reached only on foot or by mule. The city was mapped, photographed, and… pillaged. In 1951 an airstrip was constructed at the site, marking the beginning of a new adventure.

The best way to experience Tikal is to climb to the top of the Temple of the Two-Headed Serpent, which dominates the site, in the early morning. There, sixty-five meters up, one forgets about human sacrifices and the inevitable social injustices of a civilization that held sway over vast territories between the third and ninth centuries, and focuses exclusively on the enchanting scene of the pyramids, the last vestiges of a civilization brutally wiped out in its prime, emerging through the canopy of the tropical forest. The forest is so dense and so present that it is hard to give any credence—even if it is the most plausible hypothesis—to that drought that is said to have struck the Maya civilization.

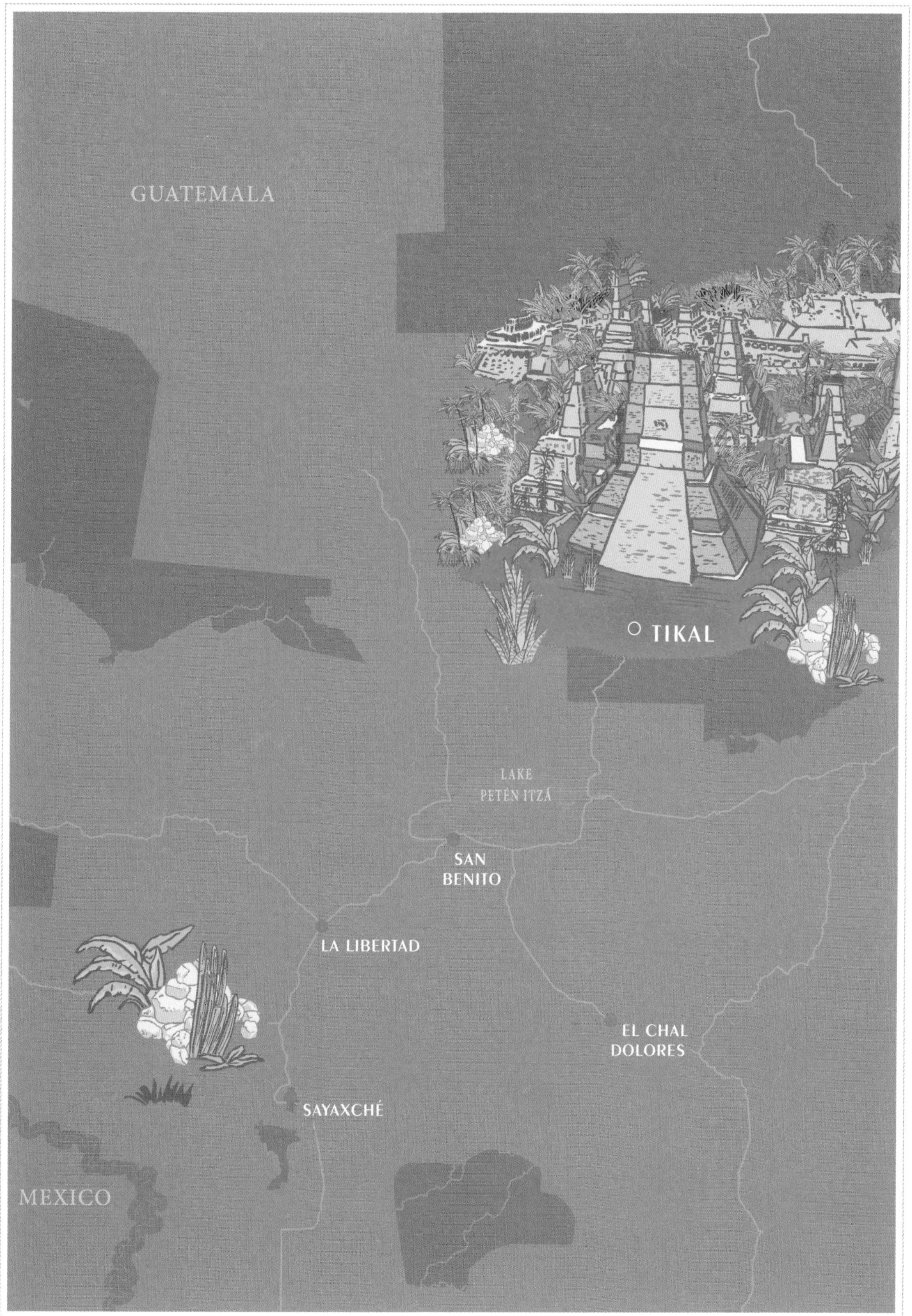

GUATEMALA

TIKAL

LAKE
PETÉN ITZÁ

SAN
BENITO

LA LIBERTAD

EL CHAL
DOLORES

SAYAXCHÉ

MEXICO

VILCABAMBA
THE LOST KINGDOM OF THE INCAS

Vilcabamba, nestling in a sacred valley covered by lush vegetation, is a mystery. Were these ruins of light-colored stone once the secret capital of the last of the Incas? Centuries after the rebellion of 1536, in which the native people sought to resist the Spanish conquistadors, this former capital continues to nurture dreams.

Tradition has it that Manco, the first of the four famous Inca rebels of Vilcabamba, chose as his center of resistance a hilly site in the shadow of the mountains. He had failed, but only by a little, in his attempt to liberate Cuzco; he had crushed the "bearded invaders" at Ongoy; and he was fleeing the troops of Almagro, who were on the march from Chile. In his secret bastion, Manco sought to recreate a small kingdom along the lines of Cuzco before it fell. For thirty-six years he launched raids against the Spanish from his hideaway. After his assassination in 1545, the Inca resistance continued under his son, the conciliatory Sayri Tupac, then under Sayri's brother, the bellicose Titu Cusi, and finally under Tupac Amaru, the fourth and last of the Incas of Vilcabamba, who remains a symbol of native resistance in Latin America to this day. In 1572 a punitive expedition led by the viceroy of Peru, incensed at the assassination of a Spanish diplomat, sealed Vilcabamba's fate. The Spanish artillery got the better of the Incas, but Tupac Amaru was able to flee after first setting his small kingdom on fire. Disdaining the warrior's burned-out city, the triumphant Spanish founded the settlement of Vilcabamba la Nueva in a more hospitable site. Vilcabamba la Vieja was abandoned and gradually submerged by an ocean of greenery.

Curiously enough, although the facts have been securely established, the precise location of the capital city of the last of the Incas was never recorded. Was this a deliberate oversight on the part of the triumphant Spanish in order to avoid transforming the place into a symbol? Either way, knowledge of a "lost city of the Incas" persisted, and in the nineteenth century a number of expeditions were launched in an attempt to locate it. Choquequirao, Machu Picchu, and Espíritu Pampa were all considered as possible sites, but these candidates were either too far north, had never been consumed by fire, or were on the wrong river. And the debate is far from over. In 1966, explorers found evidence of a fire at Espíritu Pampa and set out on their return journey convinced they had finally unearthed it. Ten years later, a Peruvian archaeologist discovered an unexplored site in the heart of the jungle forty kilometers north of Machu Picchu. He pointed to evidence of Inca occupation and claimed the place was Manco's final refuge. Since then, Choquequirao has begun to be accepted by archaeologists as the location of the secret capital of the last of the Incas. Who, then, inhabited Vilcabamba la Vieja?

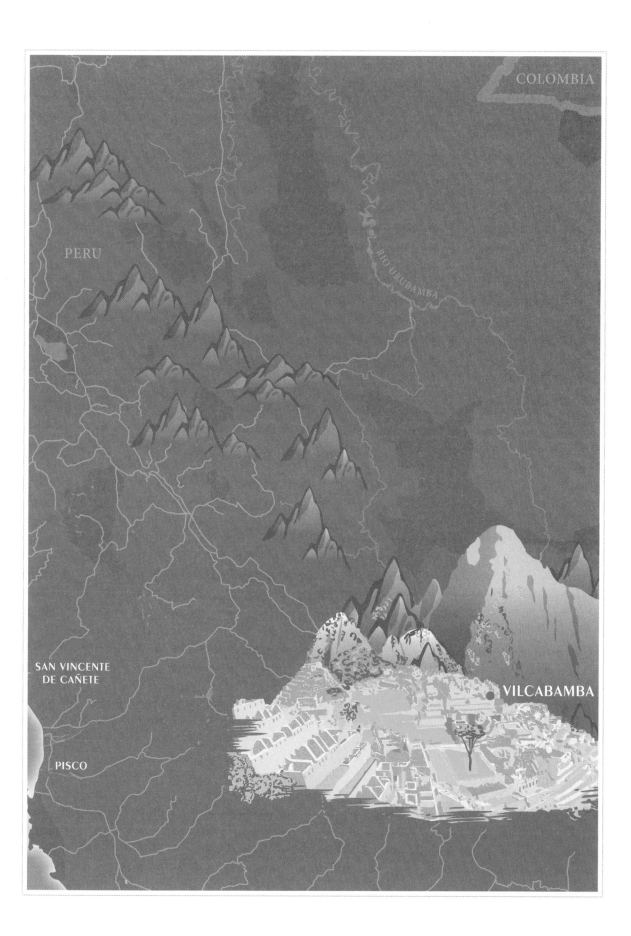

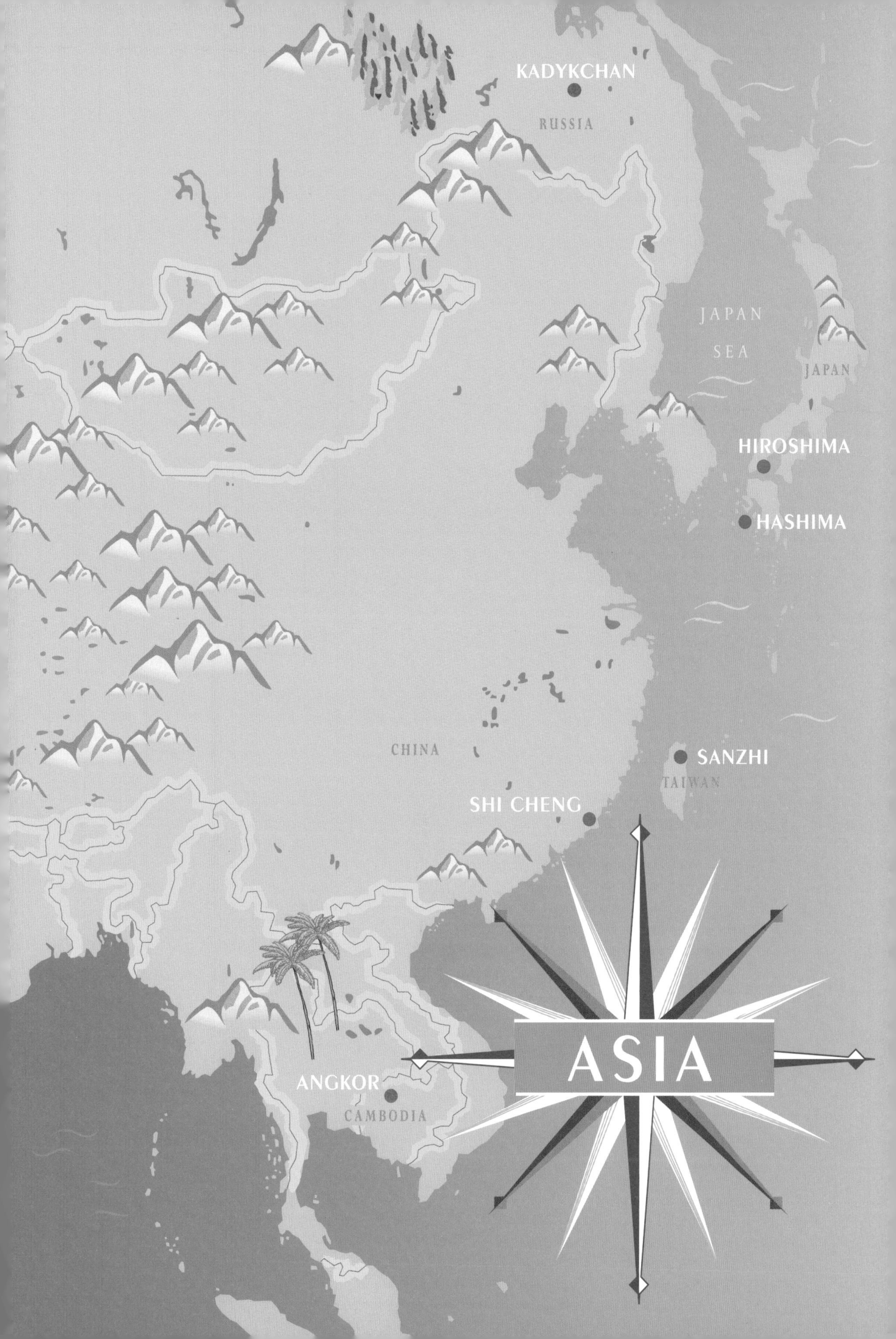

KADYKCHAN

RUSSIA

JAPAN
SEA

JAPAN

HIROSHIMA

HASHIMA

CHINA

SANZHI

TAIWAN

SHI CHENG

ASIA

ANGKOR

CAMBODIA

AZERBAIJAN · 39°59′N, 46°57′E

AGDAM
A STRATEGIC ANNIHILATION

To stroll through Agdam is an unsettling experience. Is it the silence? Is it the contrast between the sinister atmosphere of the devastated city and the natural beauty that surrounds it? It is difficult to believe that as recently as 1993, 160,000 people lived on this plain ringed by mountains. Eroded statues now preside over deserted squares, untamed vegetation cracks the asphalt, rusty tanks litter the streets, and goats graze among the apartment blocks and collective factories inherited from the Soviet days. The goatherds are presumably not far away, but in the city, not a soul stirs. At the bend in a road, a mural depicting typical Azerbaijani music making and dancing, arts outlawed under the Communist regime, can still be made out on the façade of a house that must once have been the home of a comfortably off Armenian family. Emerging from the motionless chaos, the twin minarets of the mosque—the only building not to have been bombarded—stand unscathed in apparent defiance of human folly. Agdam, nicknamed the "White City" because of the color of its stone, was obliterated almost from one day to the next in 1993 as the result of a bombardment by Armenian troops, the culmination of a conflict that had been brewing in the region for decades.

Since the eighteenth century, the city of Agdam, located in the mountainous region of Nagorno-Karabakh, a highly strategic region on the borders of Azerbaijan, Iran, and Armenia, had been an advance position of the Armenian army. So strategic was this zone that the ensuing centuries saw a succession of powers—Russian, Turkish, British, Soviet (after 1919)—try to assert their authority over it. In the twentieth century, numerous uprisings, notably by the Azeri and Armenian populations, precipitated the slow death, both cultural and economic, of a city coveted to excess. The disintegration of the Soviet regime exacerbated the tensions that had been latent throughout the region ever since the disastrous ethnic redrawing under Stalin. In 1991, diplomatic relations between Armenia and Azerbaijan, both of which possessed mighty arsenals thanks to the Soviet legacy, deteriorated. This led to a violent conflict between the two nations, resulting in the destruction of Agdam in July 1993. Ever since that spring, the people of the city had been counting the days. By the time Armenian troops entered Agdam, in order to seize arms, munitions, and food, the inhabitants had fled, without having had time to secure their homes. After pillaging both residences and public buildings, the Armenian armed forces shelled and destroyed the entire city with the deliberate aim of leaving only ruins behind. Their objective? To turn the place into a buffer zone in case of any new conflict. As a result, there is little chance of Agdam reviving anytime soon.

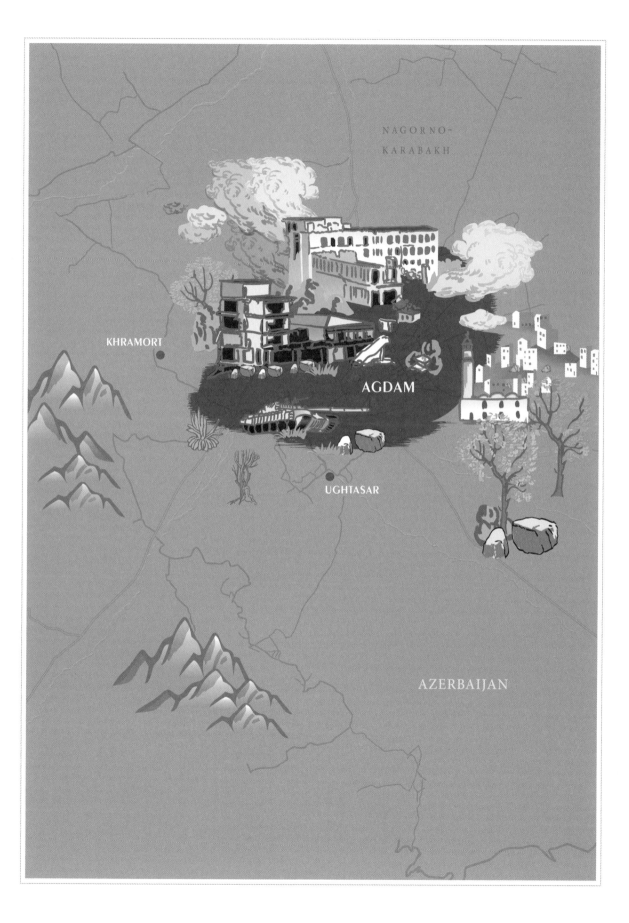

NAGORNO-
KARABAKH

KHRAMORT

AGDAM

UGHTASAR

AZERBAIJAN

CAMBODIA · 13°26′N, 103°50′E

ANGKOR
A KINGDOM OF MYSTERIES

Despite the wealth of available literature concerning the former capital of the kingdom of Cambodia, the place still holds many secrets. Covering approximately a thousand square kilometers, the ancient city has nevertheless been excavated, explored, surveyed, and decoded hundreds of times since the nineteenth century. Is it the poetic quality of the place that inspires such a host of romantic theories about Angkor's birth, heyday, and decline? To some extent, no doubt. The historians agree on certain points, however: in the ninth century A.D., during the early days of the Khmer dynasty founded by Jayavarman II, the royal city is believed to have dominated the entire central area of present-day Cambodia. An adherent of Indian culture and follower of Shaivism, the monarch introduced the cult of the divine power of the king, the god-king symbolized by the temple-mountain. At its peak, the city boasted some 750,000 inhabitants, but the collapse of the Khmer Empire—due, as so often is the case, to a combination of causes—precipitated an irreversible decline. Starting in the fifteenth century, the city was struck by a succession of extended floods and droughts. The ingenious irrigation system that had enabled Angkor to prosper

Three million tourists visit the ancient capital of the kingdom of Cambodia each year

over the centuries had deteriorated and no longer protected the crops. In addition to these ecological reasons, other contributory factors include a weakening of royal power, attacks by neighboring empires, and an outbreak of the Black Death. By the time the site was discovered by European missionaries in the sixteenth century, it was virtually deserted. It is not difficult to imagine the stupefaction of these visitors upon seeing the immense ruins, invaded by tropical vegetation and composed of blocks of sandstone green with lichen: ruined palaces, towers, temples, and statues and bas-reliefs of warriors, elephants, princes, and gods.

This forest of stones, whose magnificence leaves no one unmoved, can be said to have been properly discovered and introduced to the Western world by travelers at the end of the nineteenth century. Scientific expeditions were subsequently undertaken that gradually exposed and studied Angkor. In the 1920s the site started to become an important tourist destination and suffered periodic damage and pillaging. In 1923 the Malraux affair brought the misdeeds of such unscrupulous Westerners to widespread attention. The young avant-garde French writer had transported blocks of sculpted stone

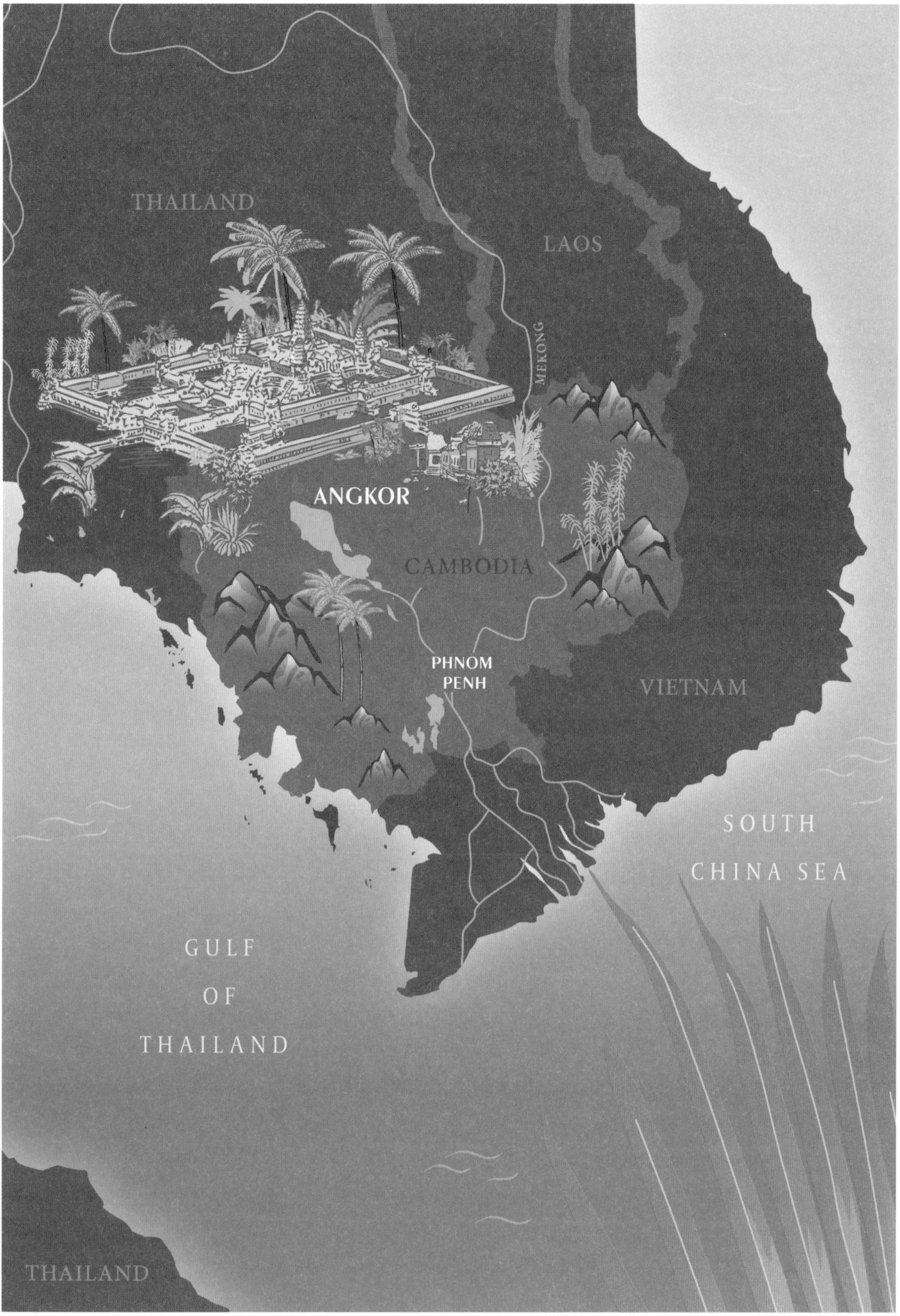

THAILAND
LAOS
MEKONG
ANGKOR
CAMBODIA
PHNOM PENH
VIETNAM
SOUTH CHINA SEA
GULF OF THAILAND
THAILAND

The forest of stones

continues to pose

numerous questions,

in particular concerning

its genesis, with evidence

of Bronze Age activity

having recently been

discovered at the site

from the temple of Banteay Srei to Phnom Penh with the intention of shipping them to France. He was arrested, though not ultimately tried, and forced to hand over the pieces to the Cambodian state.

A century later, the pillaging of the site (a sad price paid for its popularity) continues, despite the inauguration of a special police force tasked with combating the problem. In order to protect this fragile jewel from the crowds of visitors on the one hand and natural deterioration on the other, more than thirty international teams are now working side by side, in a model of international cooperation and diplomacy, on the main edifices. The forest of stones continues to pose numerous questions, in particular concerning its genesis. Evidence of Bronze Age activity has recently been uncovered, and earth remote sensing has revealed a hitherto unsuspected quantity of wooden structures, pools, and canals, astounding archaeologists and demonstrating that this outstandingly romantic place, listed in 1992 as a UNESCO World Heritage Site, still has the capacity to surprise.

The three million tourists, mainly of Asian origin, who visit Angkor each year are a testament to the ongoing appeal of the place. In addition to visiting and marveling at Angkor Thom, the last city to be built at the site, and the famous Angkor Wat, the city-temple and masterpiece of classical Khmer art converted into a Buddhist temple in the fourteenth century, these visitors also discover, to their considerable surprise, that Angkor has not given itself over completely to the worship of money—thanks to the 120,000 or so inhabitants who help to look after the site while also keeping the local craft traditions alive, and above all to the many Buddhist monks who make the pilgrimage to Angkor Wat each year. The destiny of this city founded by Jayavarman II may have changed, but it has kept a part of its soul intact.

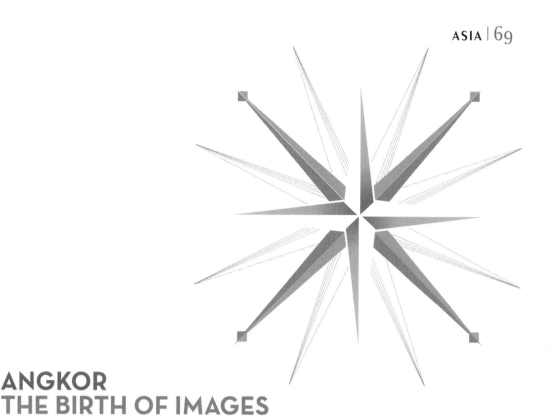

ANGKOR
THE BIRTH OF IMAGES

Claude Farrère, in *L'Illustration* (1931), wrote: "Here, then, are the temples that for so long appeared to our imagination as fabulous visions. Here are the courses of stone, the foundations, the colonnades, the extraordinary domes resembling annulated tiaras." At Angkor as at Teotihuacán and Tikal, the discovery of lost civilizations was a source of wonder to nineteenth-century adventurers. However, each "discoverer" interpreted these new worlds in his own way. The armchair traveler who learned of Angkor from the accounts of French missionaries or the sinologist Jean-Pierre Abel-Rémusat, for example, was unable to gain a particularly clear picture of the site. It was not until the engravings of the remarkable drawings by the Frenchman Henri Mouhot were published in 1863 that readers were presented with a precise, though at the same time romantic, vision of Angkor. Also dating from this period, the photographs of the Scotsman John Thomson, used by the scholar James Fergusson in his *History of Architecture in All Countries*, offer a different vision of Khmer art. This marked the opening of a new chapter. Thanks to these images, individual adventures were succeeded by "official" expeditions.

IRAQ · 32°32′N, 44°25′E

BABYLON
DYING A SECOND DEATH

The Tower of Babel, the Hanging Gardens, Queen Semiramis, King Nebuchadnezzar—the Old Testament accounts of Babylon's legend and history have endowed the city with a mythical prestige. Located at the heart of Iraq, this ancient Mesopotamian city bathed by the Euphrates is situated a hundred or so kilometers south of Baghdad. It was founded by Semiramis, the warrior queen and builder, claim the authors of classical Greece. She is said to have equipped the city with long ramparts and bedecked its enormous palace with the Hanging Gardens, which are ranked among the Seven Wonders of the Ancient World. But did they really exist? Archaeologists have never found the slightest trace of them. As for Semiramis, she seems to have been a composite of two Assyrian queens. Another founding myth is the Tower of Babel. According to the Bible, it was here that a vastly tall tower was constructed with the aim of reaching up to the heavens. Upon seeing it, God decided to punish the perpetrators. Instead of speaking the same language, as they had hitherto, the people began to speak in different tongues and, no longer able to understand one another, scattered over the face of the earth. Did the idea for this fantastic tower derive from the very high ziggurat that really did exist at Babylon? It remains a mystery.

Setting aside these fantastical stories, in reality the city goes back to around the beginning of the second millennium B.C. This, at least, was when its kings asserted themselves through successes on the battlefield and transformed the city into a major

political and religious center that experienced its apogee around the seventh and sixth centuries B.C., when the kingdom stretched from the borders of present-day Turkey to the fringes of Persia and Egypt. Conquered in succession by the Persians, Alexander the Great, and various foreign dynasties, Babylon subsequently forfeited its hegemony. Its decline continued for centuries, and by the time the Roman emperor Trajan passed through in A.D. 115, he saw more ruins than inhabitants. All that survived was the myth of a city as repeatedly described in the Bible, which present it as the archetype of the immoral metropolis: Babylon, the "mother of harlots and abominations," proclaims the book of Revelation. Excavations undertaken in the nineteenth century revealed that the remains are scattered over a thousand hectares. A century later, as in Leptis Magna, archaeology was used for political ends. When Saddam Hussein seized power, he tried to make Babylon a vehicle for his propaganda. In 1987 he launched the first festival of Babylon, which was named, in all modesty, "From Nebuchadnezzar to Saddam Hussein."

Since then, the Gulf War, the invasion of Iraq by the United States, and the fall of Saddam Hussein and the ensuing troubles have seriously endangered the remains. Today the country has other priorities and the very survival of this vast field of ruins threatened by the convulsions of the contemporary world remains in doubt. The powerful and much-feared Babylon seems in danger of dying a second death.

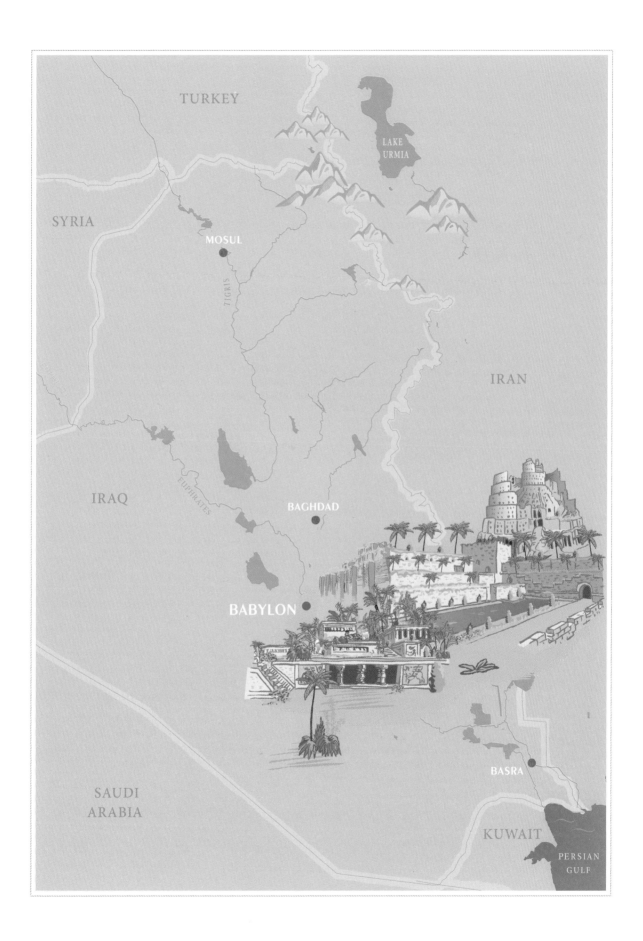

IRAN · 29°06′N, 58°21′E

BAM
THE VANISHED CITADEL

With its sixty-six towers, its interminable crenelated walls with scallop-shaped merlons, and its maze of streets and walkways surmounted by arches and domes, Bam is an amazing citadel isolated in the midst of the desert mountains. Extending over more than six square kilometers, this city-fortress, an important oasis on the silk and spice routes, is no mirage though. Established at least 2,500 years ago in the vast desert of southeastern Iran, the city was built entirely of palm trunks and adobe, which are molded mud bricks dried in the sun. It is the largest ensemble of buildings of this type in the world. Improved and reinforced over the course of the centuries, Bam has been intermittently attacked, destroyed, and rebuilt throughout its history. In the thirteenth century, when Marco Polo cites the city as an example of "castles and cities with strong walls of mud, lofty and thick," in his book *The Marvels of the World*, Bam had only recently recovered from the devastating passage of Genghis Khan. The city's final reconstruction dates from the Safavid dynasty, which lasted from the sixteenth to the eighteenth centuries. Bam consists of a military fortress built on a rise, surrounded by a walled settlement in the manner of Europe's medieval

*The ideal setting
for a dreamlike story
about the passing of time
and thwarted hopes*

cities. Until the middle of the nineteenth century, the fortress, which comprises a high watchtower, a mill, barracks, and a palace, housed the governors' district. The old city, which was abandoned by many of its residents after 1722, the year of the Afghan invasion, numbers some four hundred houses, many of which are equipped with the "wind catcher" or ventilator tower (*badgir*) typical of Persian architecture. It possessed a school, a bazaar, bakeries, public baths, stables, mosques, a caravanserai, and a *zurkhaneh* (a gymnasium dedicated to traditional wrestling), as well as various parks containing sufficient livestock to sustain the city through the long months of a siege.

Curiously enough, in the middle of the nineteenth century, Bam was completely abandoned by its inhabitants, who established a new settlement not far away, on the site of today's modern city. The reasons for this desertion of the city are a complete mystery. At the beginning of the twentieth century, Bam embarked on a new life with the arrival of tourists, both Iranian and international, curious to see this architectural jewel for themselves. In the 1950s the government applied itself to the task of reconstructing the city, in some places giving the walls the artificial freshness of a

newly molded sand castle while nevertheless respecting the traditional materials and techniques.

The people of Iran still remember the fateful morning in July 2003 when, in precisely seven minutes, the age-old citadel was reduced to rubble by a violent earthquake, which also claimed the lives of more than thirty thousand inhabitants of the modern city. The tremor destroyed everything, starting with the reconstructions, whose design had failed to take the seismic risks into account. All that was left were collapsed walls, broken domes, and orphaned arches and columns exposed to the harsh effects of the sand and dust whipped up by the wind.

Like the modern city, which had to be rebuilt from scratch, the citadel was the subject of an international rescue operation involving the collaboration, which continues today, of many countries, in particular Japan, Italy, and France. With the mud brick factory

Bam was to be attacked, destroyed, and rebuilt several times over the course of the centuries

working at full capacity and scaffolding burgeoning between the walls, within ten years of the earthquake the most emblematic elements of the structure had already been restored to their former aspect. A complete renovation is not, however, on the agenda, at least as things stand today. This would harm the authenticity of the site, and furthermore, the experts who have been poring over the remains have discovered even older vestiges dating back some six thousand years. They have requested that these previously undiscovered remains be preserved from any further damage that might be caused by the construction of buildings on top of them.

Strolling along the restored ramparts today, one is struck by the truly enchanting view of the monochrome city streets below, shaded by eucalyptus trees, and the desert beyond. In its new life, the fortress will remain a fascinating film set forever.

In its new life, the fortress

will remain a fascinating

film set forever

INDIA · 27°06′N, 77°40′E

FATEHPUR SIKRI
EPHEMERAL CAPITAL

Its pink domes standing out against a milky white sky, the ancient Mughal city of Fatehpur Sikri rises above an immense plain dotted with mustard fields. Emperor Akbar, having reached twenty-six years of age, was worried about not having an heir. He consulted a hermit reputed to be wise, who predicted that a son would be born to him. One year later the prediction came true. Wanting to keep the holy man by his side, Akbar decided to move his capital to the exact spot where the sage lived, on the Sikri Ridge, a rocky plateau southwest of Agra. Work began on the construction of the city in 1572.

Subtly blending Arab, Persian, and Hindu influences, the capital reflects the interests of Akbar, an enlightened and deeply pious monarch with an interest in the arts. And if the austerity of the bare stone causes visitors to forget the time when these palaces resounded with the clatter of arms and the buzz of the court, the architectural fantasies of this inspired place underline the sophistication of Mughal culture. Protected by an encircling wall and dispersed around a vast esplanade are winter and summer residences, the palace of Akbar's wives (the first was Christian, the second Hindu, and the third Muslim), mosques, terraces, labyrinthine passages, and pavilions and kiosks shaded by awnings—and all this graced by columns, capitals, and elaborate windows whose pink stone is worked as finely as wood. The organization of space is so ingenious that Fatehpur Sikri was to have a major influence on Indian urban planning, notably that of Old Delhi.

For a period of twelve years, from 1573 to 1585, Akbar lived here with his court and harem before leaving to confront the Afghan tribes, at which time he moved his residence to Lahore. For a few months in 1619, Fatehpur Sikri became the seat of the court once again when Jahangir, Akbar's son, took refuge here in order to escape an epidemic of the plague in Agra. However, several years of drought had got the better of the artificial lake and reservoirs created decades before. Without enough water to satisfy its needs, the court abandoned the city for good, leaving it to slowly fall into ruins. After a long period of neglect, the former capital was eventually rediscovered at the very end of the nineteenth century. Inhabited by monkeys, squirrels, and crows alone, the phantom city extends in all directions around the tomb of the hermit, a masterpiece of carved marble. This has pride of place in the empty court of the great mosque, and rightly so, because had it not been for the holy man, Fatehpur Sikri would never have been built.

KALADEO
PARK

AGRA

FATEHPUR SIKRI

UTTAR
PRADESH

GANGES RIVER

DHOLPUR

GAMBHIR RIVER

TURKEY · 40°01′N, 34°38′E

HATTUSA
THE CAPITAL OF A FORGOTTEN KINGDOM

Hattusa is more mysterious and less well known than any other ancient city. Indeed, it is almost improbable that it is known at all, since for a long time Hattusa survived in human memory only thanks to a brief mention in Genesis. But a surprise discovery was to bring it to the attention of the world. In 1834, while on an expedition to Asia Minor, a French archaeologist uncovered some remains near the village of Bogazkale at the heart of a mountainous region in central Anatolia. He believed he had discovered the ancient city of Tavium referred to by Herodotus and Strabo. He was wrong: what he had found were the remains of Hattusa, the capital of the kingdom of the Hittites, as confirmed by a collection of tablets discovered at the site of Amarna in Egypt in 1880.

It was in this remote corner of Anatolia, near the Kizil River, that the capital of one of the most powerful kingdoms in the Middle East once stood. Hattusa was a religious center of the utmost importance and a commercial crossroads through which passed minerals and textiles. Rigorous excavations embarked upon by a German archaeologist in 1906 uncovered a veritable treasure trove: thousands of tablets in cuneiform script that revealed how the diplomacy, politics, and religious and judicial systems of the Hittite civilization functioned. However, these tablets do not tell the whole story, offering no clues about the demise of the city prior to the end of the Hittite Empire. At the end of the nineteenth century, the Hittite people and their capital, Hattusa, had only just been discovered, and nothing was known about their culture. Today, one mystery in particular remains: how, having controlled numerous vassal states between Anatolia and Syria, did Hattusa disappear barely a century after attaining the height of its splendor and power in the thirteenth century B.C.? Archaeologists are intrigued by visible signs of destruction on its monuments. Regularly invaded during the course of a singularly chaotic history, it is possible that the city was ultimately laid to waste by an enemy. All that is known for certain, however, is that Hattusa was on the decline and had already been largely abandoned in favor of another capital when it was destroyed by invaders.

Today, the site is as impressive for its mountainous setting as it is for its excavated or reassembled monuments. Built on a plateau punctuated by hills, at almost 1,200 meters above sea level, Hattusa must have been a breathtaking sight at the peak of its

Hattusa was the capital of one of the most powerful kingdoms in the Middle East

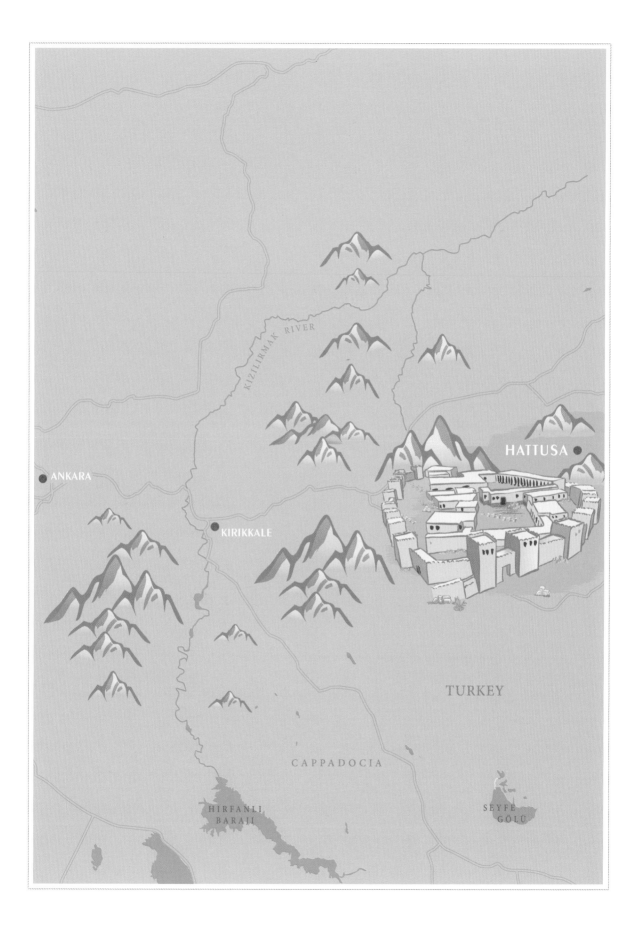

splendor. Whereas nowadays the sparse vegetation struggles to break through the stony ground, back then the landscape was less arid. Since the start of the excavations, archaeologists have unearthed a complex covering more than 160 hectares. Of the encircling double walls punctuated by square towers, which once had a circumference of six kilometers, various sections, consisting of enormous, unadorned stones, have survived. The city's ground plan can still be made out: at the center, on a steep rise known as Büyükalle, stood the great fortress, protecting the royal apartments and dominating the lower town. This was the first site to be occupied, in all likelihood as early as the third millennium B.C. Its first inhabitants were the Hatti people, who were later subjugated by the Hittites. Extending to the south of Büyükalle is the upper town, constructed much later, as evidenced by its foundations dating from the thirteenth century, when Hattusa regained its position as the Hittites' capital after being briefly eclipsed by another town. Also at this time, temples sprang up all over the city. At the southern extremity of the city, the part most difficult to defend, was a particularly impressive structure: the Yerkapi mound. This was a gigantic man-made earthwork, more than sixty meters wide at its base and crowned with mud brick ramparts

The site is as impressive for its mountainous setting as it is for its excavated monuments

resting on a course of stone. A section of this structure has recently been reconstructed and boasts massive crenelated towers. A number of the city gates are still visible. These are the Lion Gate; the Sphinx Gate, which owes its name to the flanking statues of the hybrid creature with the head of a woman, the body of a lion, and curious wings resembling those of a bird of prey; and the so-called Gate of the King, decorated with a bas-relief representing a god armed with an ax and a sword. Inevitably, time has taken its toll, and the sculptures that are still visible appear to be of only rudimentary workmanship. They nevertheless allow visitors to imagine the pomp of royal and religious processions, the clatter of weapons as the Hittite armies prepared to leave to do battle far away (for example against the troops of Ramesses II at Kadesh), and the incessant to-ing and fro-ing of the merchants' caravans as they resupplied this city designed to withstand a siege.

Forgotten, rediscovered, misunderstood, and finally revealed for what it really was, Hattusa, which was inscribed as a UNESCO World Heritage Site, along with the neighboring sanctuary of Yazilikaya, in 1986, has yet to give up its final secrets, and the story of its downfall remains an enigma to this day.

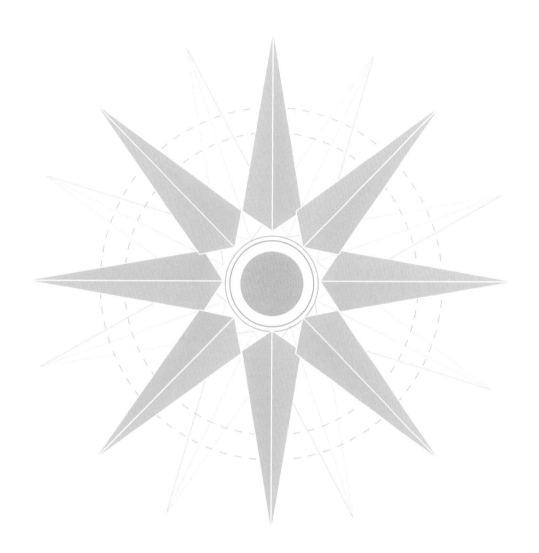

Hattusa was inscribed
as a UNESCO
World Heritage Site
in 1986

JAPAN · 34°23′N, 132°27′E

HIROSHIMA

OVERCOMING TRAGEDY

"You've seen nothing in Hiroshima . . . " This famous phrase from the Alain Resnais film *Hiroshima Mon Amour* is uttered continually by the Japanese actor Eiji Okada. It expresses the awful reality that horror cannot be shared, that it is indescribable for anyone who has not lived through it. Can there be anyone unfamiliar with the name of this coastal city on Honshu Island, a strategic industrial center during the Second World War that was obliterated in a few seconds on the morning of April 6, 1945, by the first atomic bomb to be dropped in wartime? It is impossible to forget the image of a giant radioactive mushroom cloud shooting into the sky, attaining an altitude of ten thousand meters in just two minutes and unleashing a shock wave that destroyed everything in its path. The city—built mainly of wood—was transformed into a vast, muddy plain, bare but for the odd concrete structure and a few skeletal, cindered trees. The unbearable images of survivors with atrocious burns, the so-called *hibakusha*, are impossible to forget, as is the terrible toll, over the ensuing years, of cancer sufferers and babies born with deformities, testifying to the folly of a world in which science no longer necessarily means progress, but destruction, too.

Today, having risen again over its debris, Hiroshima resembles any other Japanese metropolis. Numbering a million inhabitants, compared to a little over three hundred thousand—including thousands of Chinese and Korean forced laborers—before it was destroyed, the city is built on a grid system and is traversed by several rivers that converge as they approach the sea. Its noisy major arteries, lined with glass and steel office blocks; its side streets, accommodating the city's nightlife; and its peaceful modern residential districts rub shoulders with 1950s reconstructions of its historic buildings. Thus the city castle, originally erected in the 1590s, a massive five-story structure typical of the feudal era, with roofs of curved tiles, was rebuilt after the Second World War in reinforced concrete. Various other monuments are more directly evocative of the suffering of the victims. These are concentrated in the Peace Memorial Park: the emblematic Genbaku Dome, a former exhibition hall built of brick whose central dome has been maintained in its damaged state, and the cenotaph designed by architect Kenzo Tange, where the names of all those known to have died in the bombing or from illnesses caused by it are contained in a stone coffin and added to year after year. Some seventy years on, the first nuclear tragedy in the history of mankind is not about to be forgotten.

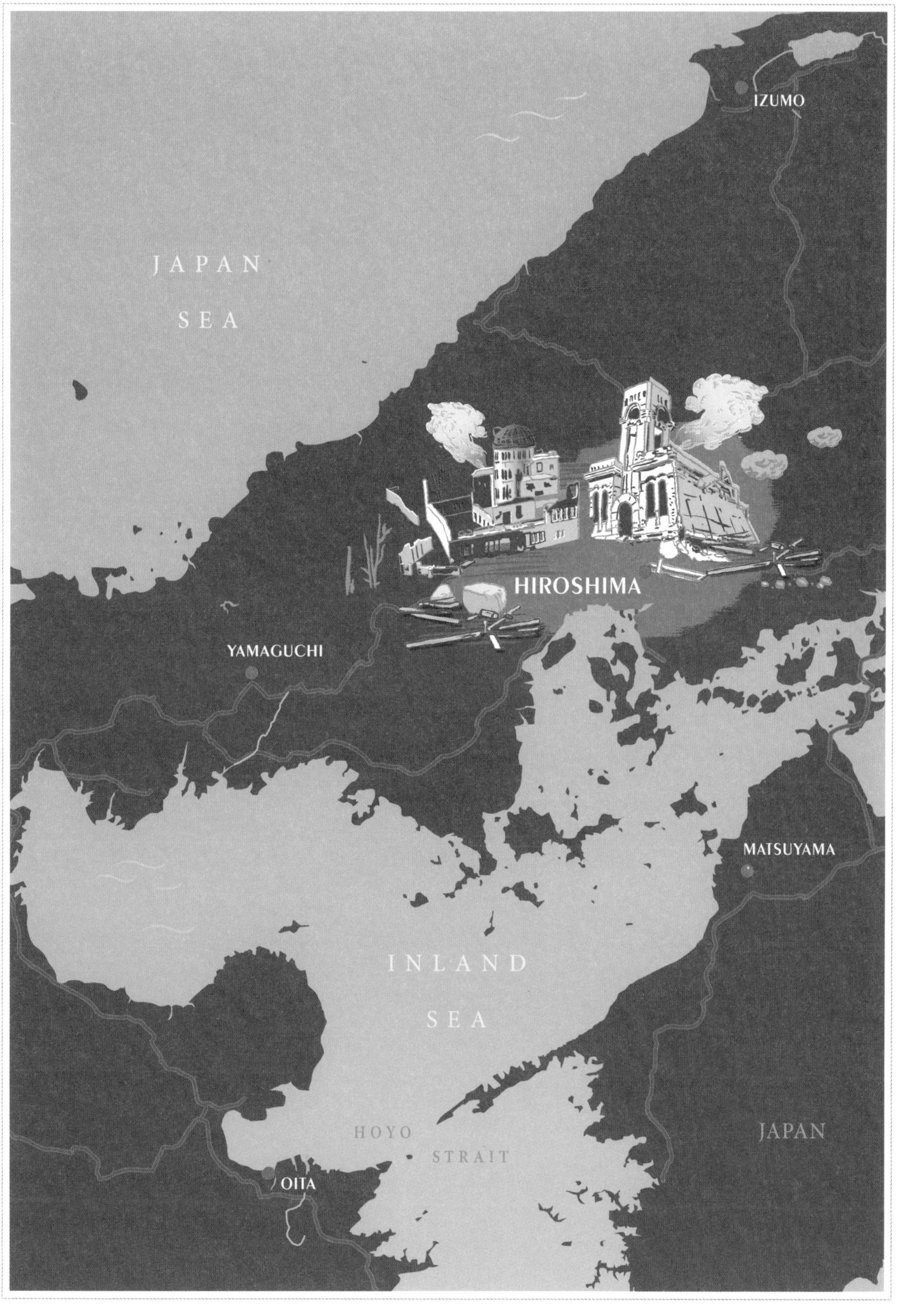

JAPAN

SEA

IZUMO

HIROSHIMA

YAMAGUCHI

MATSUYAMA

INLAND

SEA

JAPAN

HOYO

STRAIT

OITA

JAPAN · 32°37′N, 129°44′E

HASHIMA
"BATTLESHIP ISLAND"

Upon seeing the lair of Silva, the villain played by Javier Bardem in the 2012 James Bond movie *Skyfall*, some noticed its resemblance to a real place located off the coast of Japan, a tiny island battered by the waves of the Pacific Ocean. Was this perhaps a penitentiary surrounded by water and therefore impossible to break out of? A fortress built to keep watch over the hundred or so uninhabited islands in its vicinity? An enormous vessel run aground following some unknown disaster? Hashima, the island also known to the Japanese as Gunkanjima, meaning "Battleship Island," is none of these. The story begins at the start of the nineteenth century, with the discovery on the island of coal deposits that would alter the island's destiny.

With the dawn of the Meiji era (1868–1912), Japan suddenly entered the modern world, and coal, a precious resource essential to the economic development of the empire, became an object of desire. In 1890 the Mitsubishi Corporation, which had recently entered a phase of all-out diversification, acquired this pebble (measuring barely six hectares) in the ocean along with its perimeter sea wall and wharves, and set to work exploiting its coal and populating the place with miners. These workers had to endure extremely harsh working conditions and a Spartan life for them and their families. In view of the scarcity of land, some of it reclaimed from the sea, they were housed in tall blocks whose apartments were more like monastic cells. The collective kitchens and sanitary facilities, on the other hand, provided a semblance of comfort. All the buildings were made of concrete, a material considered at the time to be modern and revolutionary. By 1916, Hashima, which had several schools, a hospital, and many shops, numbered three thousand inhabitants and was buzzing with life. In 1941, on the eve of Japan's entry into the Second World War, the island yielded some 410,000 metric tons of coal per year. The following year, in order to replace the miners who had gone off to fight, Korean and Chinese forced laborers were brought in, many of whom perished as a result of accidents or illness. After 1945, the demand for coal was stimulated by the Korean War, as a result of which mining activity on the island intensified. By 1959, 5,300 people were living there. This represented the highest population density anywhere in the world, the equivalent of 84,100 inhabitants per square kilometer—and even more in the most urbanized portions of this minuscule territory! The island was now livelier than ever before, offering its inhabitants a wide and eclectic range of facilities, including a cinema, bars, a Buddhist temple, a Shinto shrine, and even a brothel. In order to compensate for the lack of green space, crops were planted on the roofs, creating hanging gardens. For this, soil had to

The ghost town in Skyfall really does exist— off the coast of Japan

NAKANOSHIMA ISLAND

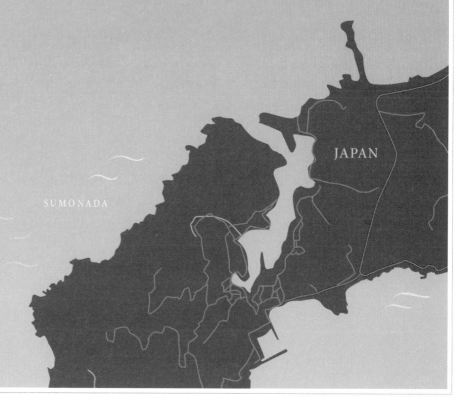

HASHIMA

AMAKUSA

SEA

SUMONADA

JAPAN

With its tight rows
of uniformly gray apartment blocks,
this strange place is reminiscent
of a Piranesi drawing

be transported to the island at considerable cost. Hashima's decline set in at the end of the 1960s, when oil started to replace coal, and mining on this speck of land in the ocean was considered too expensive. Unemployed miners started to leave the concrete isle. In 1974 it was abandoned for good when Mitsubishi closed the last working mine.

During the ensuing years, when the island was proclaimed out of bounds for security reasons, typhoons and the sea air wrought considerable damage. In 2009 a ferry started to run between the island and the mainland, dropping off visitors who were curious to see for themselves this strange place that bore more than a passing resemblance to a Piranesi drawing, with its tight rows of dilapidated, uniformly gray apartment blocks around whose feet clumps

of rampant vegetation had grown up. With space formerly at such a premium, the decaying buildings were linked by staircases and separated by narrow passages, making the island a real-life labyrinth. Providing they were prepared to brave the ever-growing piles of rubble, visitors could wander through the empty apartments, where remnants of everyday objects and furniture recalled the lives once led here. Some of these day-trippers were former inhabitants who came in search of their past. Having founded an association, these one-time Hashima residents are now trying to have the island listed as a UNESCO World Heritage Site in homage to all those who lived and suffered in this improbable place that defied the ocean.

In 2009 a ferry started
to serve the island again,
occasionally dropping off
former inhabitants
in search of their past

RUSSIA · 63°00´N, 146°57´E

KADYKCHAN
THE "LAND OF THE WHITE DEATH"

Photographs from the 1960s show a dapper little town against a background of mountains and verdant prairies. But these were merely propaganda images. A brief glimpse at a map reveals a less alluring reality. Kadykchan is located at the eastern extremity of Russia in the Kolyma region of Siberia, known for its unimaginably harsh climate. This territory is known for something else, too. For decades, the name Kadykchan was only ever uttered in hushed tones. This "land of the white death," as it was nicknamed, accommodated hundreds of thousands of prisoners in the infamous work camps or gulags introduced by Stalin. Enduring appalling living conditions and with a high rate of mortality, this unpaid workforce underwent "reeducation" through work, in this case the extraction of the fabulous riches that lie buried in the ground beneath Kolyma—gold, silver, copper, uranium, cobalt, diamonds, coal—and to which Kadykchan owed its birth at the end of the 1930s.

The town's history is typical of its kind. Next to three opencast mines, barracks were hastily thrown up by the prisoners of the gulag. This camp gradually developed into a town. The death of Stalin in 1953, followed by the relatively liberal Khrushchev regime, changed little in the lives of the now former prisoners, a majority of whom chose to remain where they were and to continue working at the mine, enduring conditions that remained extremely harsh. By the 1960s, Kadykchan numbered some ten thousand inhabitants. Although it had gradually modernized and now boasted the collective infrastructure on which socialist felicity depended, it was still a universe apart. The eventual collapse of the communist regime, the disruption to coal production following the change of regime, and the depletion of the deposits proved fatal to the town. The population had been dwindling since 1990, but soon people started to leave in droves. In 1996, a pit explosion claimed six lives. This catastrophe sounded the death knell for the mine. The Russian government suspended production and offered the remaining inhabitants meager subsidies to relocate. Having been abandoned by the rest of world, a deathly silence soon settled on Kadykchan.

Assailed by a glacial wind and disappearing for much of the year in a snowy fog, the town is now a melancholy sight, with rutted roads; dilapidated, faded apartment blocks at the foot of which children's play areas can be made out; a cultural center whose façade still displays the word *Sevodnya*, announcing the entertainment of the day; and an enormous demolished statue. Along the streets, the doors of letter boxes swing in the wind, while in the town's schools books litter the floor, serving as a poignant reminder that in this place there was once life, the laughter of children, and moments of celebration.

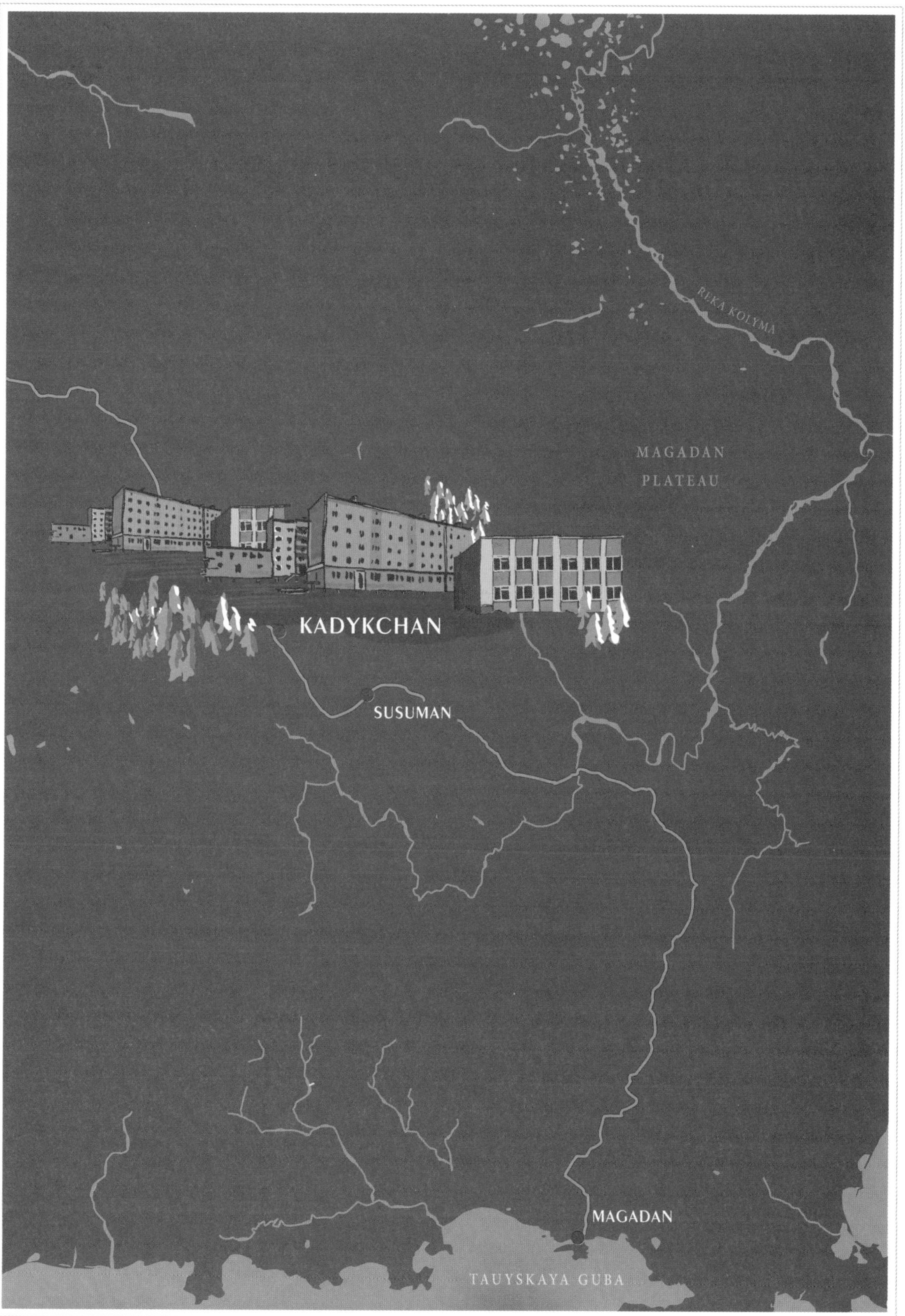

KADYKCHAN

SUSUMAN

MAGADAN
PLATEAU

REKA KOLYMA

MAGADAN

TAUYSKAYA GUBA

KANTUBEK
CONTAMINATED ZONE

Its location is improbable and its environment hostile: Kantubek is situated on Vozrozhdeniya Island, a forbidding no man's land in the middle of the Aral Sea, which is in turn surrounded by deserts. It is literally the back of beyond, but now home to a ghost town. Nobody goes to the island anymore unless they are holding the appropriate permit and are wearing a special suit of clothing. At the very most, the place will be vaguely known from the odd satellite photograph showing a lunar landscape on which a few sparse structures can be made out. Upon closer inspection, the images are not at all flattering: set in the midst of a desert landscape dotted with scrub are a collection of apartment blocks with gaping windows, wooden barracks, and dilapidated industrial installations, a chaotic ensemble of burned-out ruins, collapsed roofs, wrecked trucks, and rusted metal. The only apparently intact element is the grid pattern of the roads, lined with street lamps that have not given out any light for years and years.

Kantubek was the heart of a vast biological weapons research center

All things considered, the history of Kantubek is pretty appalling. The child of Stalinist paranoia and the Cold War, this town, which has never had more than 1,500 inhabitants, was the heart of a vast research center in which the Soviet government developed and tested its biological weapons programs.

Ever since 1936, the government had known that the island offered the ideal set of conditions for highly dangerous experiments of this kind. It benefited from a warm, dry climate, with a ground-level temperature of 6 degrees Celsius, which prevented the proliferation and dissemination of pathogenic microorganisms. A unit headed by Professor Ivan Velikanov, an eminent specialist in bacteriological warfare and the director of a Red Army–sponsored laboratory, was duly established on Vozrozhdeniya. In 1937, however, the island was evacuated, officially for security reasons, and Velikanov became a victim of Stalinist terror. He was dismissed from his duties and, some years later, executed.

In 1952 a decision was made, and ratified by the Soviet authorities, to resume the experiments. Two years later, the first installations were constructed on the island. The key facility, the laboratory for the testing of pathogenic agents, was established in the south of the island. The town of Kantubek, comprising military and civilian accommodation as well as the necessary public infrastructure, was built in the northeast, while an airport was constructed in the west. Finally, a port complex allowed boats to patrol on an ongoing basis in order to ensure the site's absolute security. Secrecy was sacrosanct. The scientists chosen to live

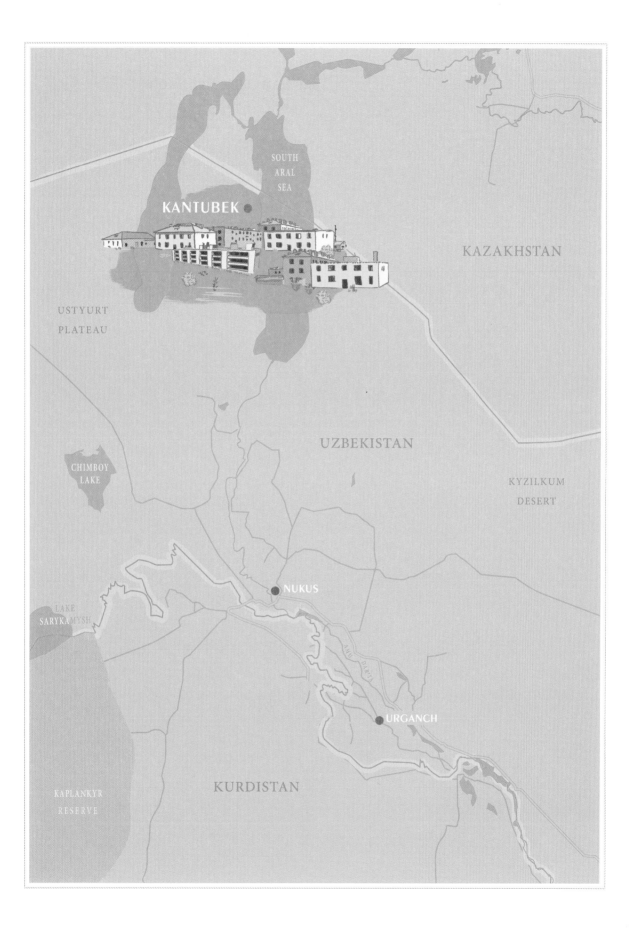

KANTUBEK

SOUTH
ARAL
SEA

KAZAKHSTAN

USTYURT
PLATEAU

UZBEKISTAN

CHIMBOY
LAKE

KYZILKUM
DESERT

LAKE
SARYKAMYSH

NUKUS

ABU DARYA

URGANCH

KAPLANKYR
RESERVE

KURDISTAN

Here, secrecy
was sacrosanct.
Nothing was to get out
about the
extremely dangerous
experiments conducted
on the island.

on the island were handpicked and risked their lives if they gave anything away about their experiments with the most dangerous pathogenic agents in the world—anthrax, botulinus toxin, typhus, brucellosis, Venezuelan equine encephalitis—any of which had the capacity to decimate populations in record time. These substances had only to be released into the atmosphere or injected into animals, which were in good supply in the experimentation zone: not only rodents but also pigs, horses, donkeys, and sheep. The pathogenic strains were administered to all and the deadly effects observed. In spite of the drastic security measures in the experimentation zone and the sensors installed all over Kantubek that subjected the inhabitants to intense medical scrutiny, it seems that a number of incidents occurred. Was a new alert the reason the town was evacuated in 1992? It remains a mystery, although the state of the apartment blocks and laboratories, which appear to have been abandoned in a hurry, suggest that this may have been the case. Today only one thing is certain: the zone has never been completely decontaminated, and stocks of biochemical agents remain on site waiting to be plundered. This situation has become all the more dangerous now that Vozrozhdeniya Island, which is today divided between Kazakhstan and Uzbekistan, has been transformed into a peninsula as a result of the gradual drying-up of the Aral Sea, with the consequence that it is now far easier to access. In 2001 the international community finally reacted. The following year a specialist team from the United States Department of Defense was dispatched to the site and neutralized between one hundred and two hundred metric tons of anthrax bacteria.

Something has at last been done, but, alas, only the minimum. Who knows what substances remain within the reach of dangerous or deranged individuals in this desolate landscape at the back of beyond?

The zone has never been
completely decontaminated
and is a disaster
waiting to be looted

KAYAKÖY

THE STONES OF EXILE

If Kayaköy is visited on a regular basis, it is only because the "ghost town," as it is referred to by the region's tour operators, is only eight kilometers away from the pulsating city of Fethiye, an extremely popular seaside resort on the Turquoise Coast. There is a striking contrast between the lively Mediterranean coast from Izmir to Antalya and the sinister atmosphere of the roofless gray stone houses of Kayaköy, whose gaping windows seem to fix the mountainous horizon with an unseeing stare. The most impressive thing about this place is the uniformity of the cube-like houses lined up along streets sprouting wild grass and fig trees whose roots miraculously insinuate themselves between the masonry despite the scarcity of water in these parts. Founded at the beginning of the seventeenth century, this small town boasted several chapels and two churches, whose erstwhile splendor is hinted at by traces of fresco and fragments of black and white mosaic tiling. Until 1923, its inhabitants, Orthodox Greeks who were descendants of the Lycians, a seafaring people thought to have arrived from Crete around 1400 B.C., reached some sort of accommodation with their Ottoman overlords and lived here peaceably alongside their Turkish neighbors. Under the Byzantine Empire they had embraced Christianity, giving rise to their nickname,

"Rums" (that is to say, Romans), and explaining the number of chapels and churches dotted around the town.

In 1923 the treaty that ended Turkey's War of Independence called for the "repatriation" of a million Anatolian Greeks to the mother country they did not know and the return to the newly formed Republic of Turkey of some four thousand Turkish Muslims living in Greece and the Balkans. Large numbers of Turks, mainly from Thessaloniki, moved into this town, then still known by its Lycian name of Karmylassos (it would later be rebaptized Kayaköy in an act of "Turkification"). The graft did not take, however, not least because of a tenacious rumor that the Greeks had cast a spell on their homes before leaving. More seriously, the disaffection of the town's new inhabitants stemmed from problems of water supply. Within a few months, these peasants, unaccustomed to such an austere life, established a new community farther down the valley. Today the only businesses are a few cafés that have opened in order to exploit the tourist trade. Their customers occasionally include Australians who have come in search of their roots. These are the descendants of "Rums" who, not wishing to be exiled to Greece, chose to make a new life for themselves on the other side of the world.

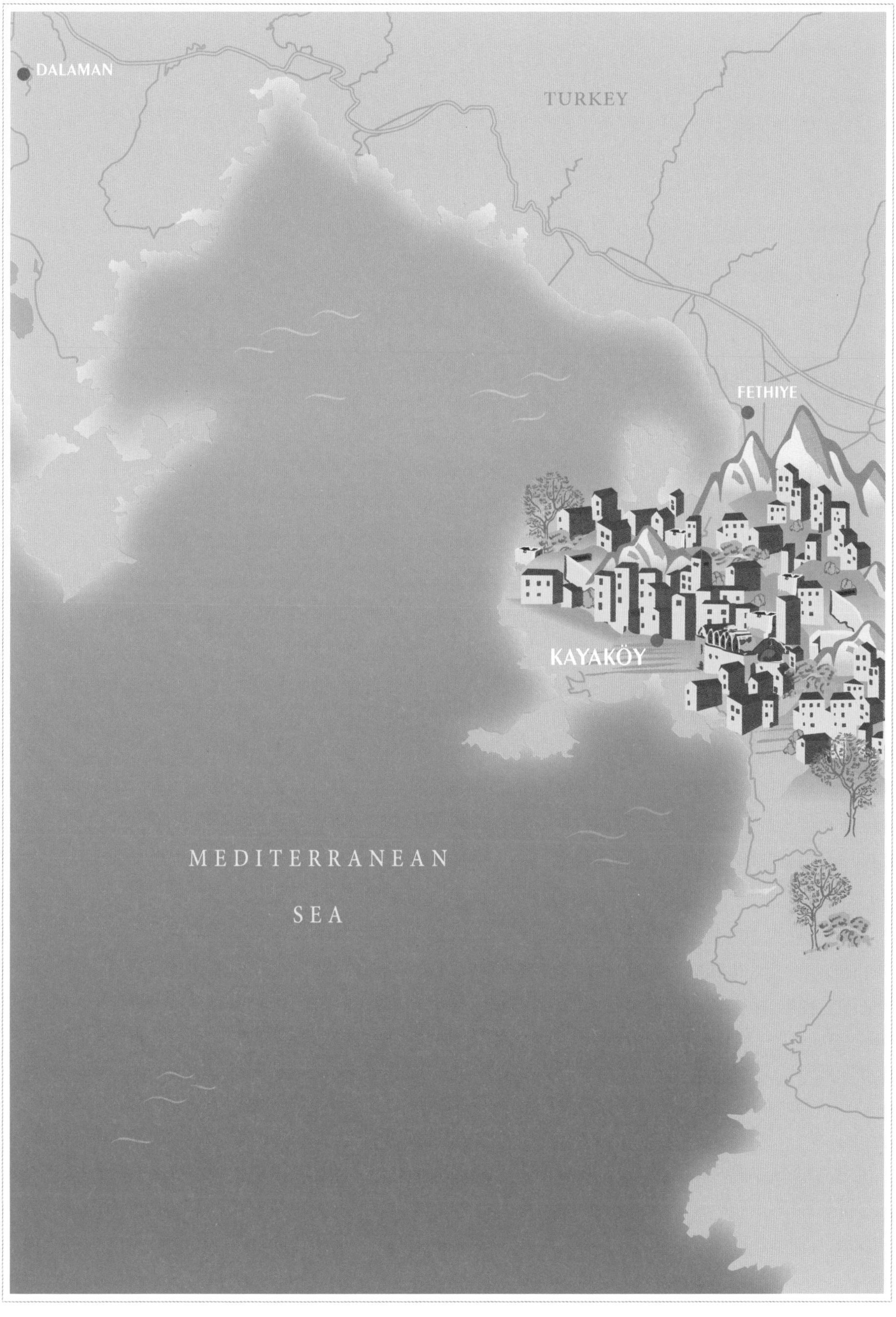

DALAMAN

TURKEY

FETHIYE

KAYAKÖY

MEDITERRANEAN

SEA

INDIA · 22°19′N, 72°24′E

LOTHAL
THE "MOUND OF THE DEAD"

It would be no exaggeration to say that Lothal, one of India's most important archaeological sites, is well and truly off the tourist trail. Situated eighty-five kilometers south of Ahmedabad, it is surrounded by the grayish fields of an alluvial plain that stretches unchanging into the distance. Admittedly, there is little here to attract the crowds—neither elaborately sculpted temples nor majestic walls. Lothal's history, however, is captivating and tells the story of the Indus civilization, India's oldest, which flourished between 3300 and 1900 B.C., during the transition from the Neolithic period to the Bronze Age. Regarded as sophisticated beyond its times, this civilization, which originated at Harappa in Pakistan, was renowned for its urban organization, its incredibly precise system of weights and measures, and its trading prowess, via both land and water. Indeed Lothal's origins are closely connected with the sea.

Around 2450 B.C., merchants seeking a base on the southern trade route came across a potters' village ideally situated on the Sabarmati River, deep in the Gulf of Khambhat. There they established a port. The locals' ingenious techniques for the production of ceramic wares and the newcomers' facility with stone and copper tools ensured more than five hundred years of prosperity. At the time of the Harappans'

Now completely landlocked, the port of Lothal is one of the oldest cities, dating from India's prehistoric era

arrival, the future Lothal was protected by a simple mud brick wall behind which vessels ran aground at low tide. The first flood, a hundred or so years later, led to a review of the entire system and the construction of a functional city and port. These were further improved after the second major flood, which occurred in 2200 B.C.. The population at this time is estimated to have been between one thousand and two thousand. The third reconstruction, in 2000 B.C., coincided with the desertion of Lothal by its elite classes and the onset of the city's decline. After the fourth inundation, in 1900 B.C., nothing remained but a few reed huts, which in turn were abandoned as the remains of the city sank into the mud and neglect.

Since 1955, seven major excavations have enabled the history of the city, marked by this succession of catastrophic floods and reconstructions, to be told. Even today, when the Sabarmati River and its tributaries have silted up the estuary and forced the sea to retreat by more than thirty kilometers, the plain, which rises no higher than ten meters above sea level, is regularly swamped during the monsoon. The smallest village perched on a hillock is transformed during the rains into an islet from which the villagers can do nothing but survey the ephemeral verdure of their wheat and

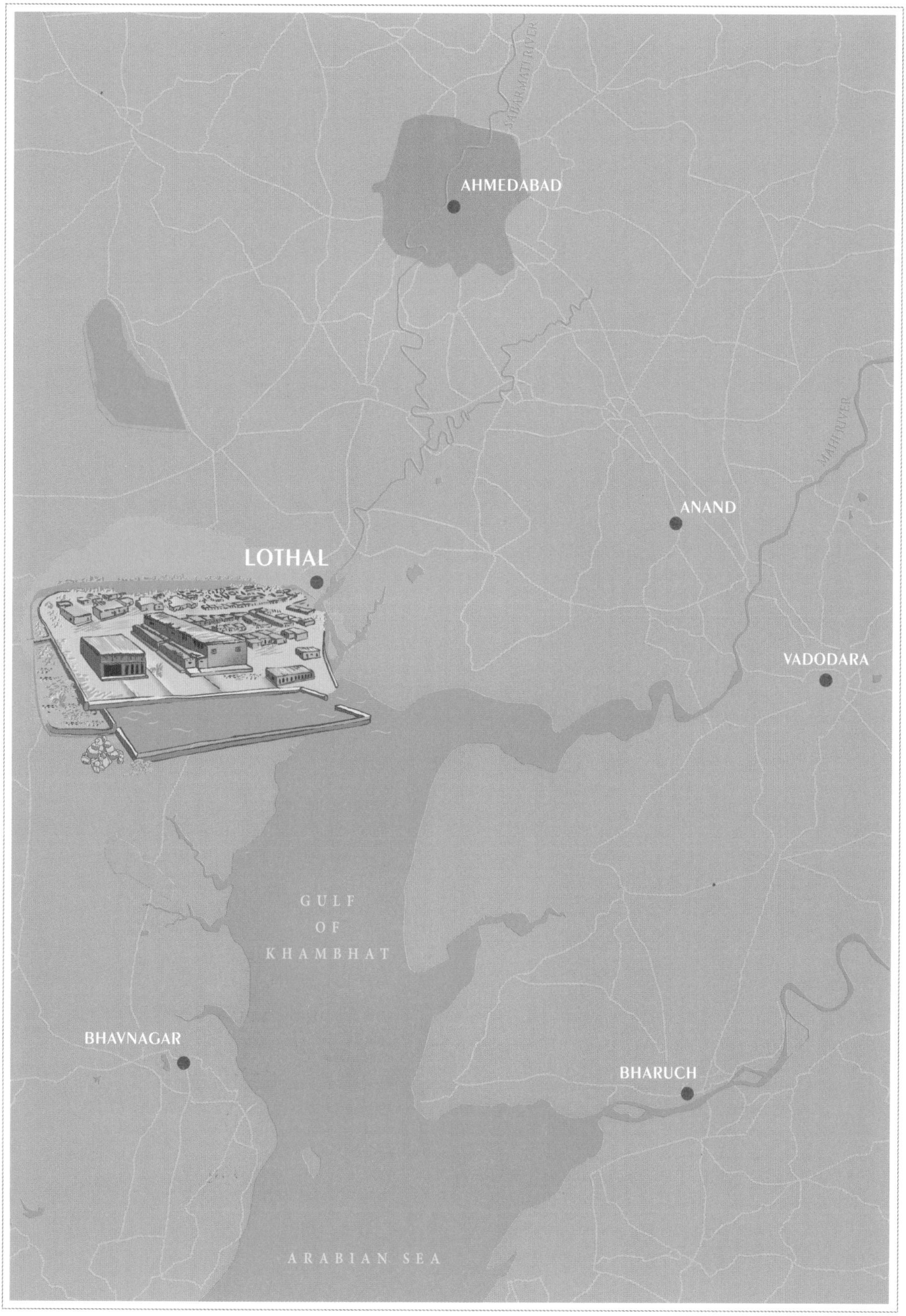

AHMEDABAD

ANAND

MAHI RIVER

SABARMATI RIVER

LOTHAL

VADODARA

GULF
OF
KHAMBHAT

BHAVNAGAR

BHARUCH

ARABIAN SEA

cotton fields. The remains that are on view today date from the city's golden age. Although it requires a degree of imagination to bring them to life, the small museum at the site offers plentiful explanations, enabling visitors to find their bearings as they pick their way through the maze of low walls of pink brick and checkerboard street layout: here, the upper town, raised on a terrace 3.5 meters high, consisting of spacious homes and vast warehouses; there, the houses and workshops of the ordinary folk. Visitors marvel at the baths in each home and the sophisticated drainage system that filters out solid waste. The sight most worthy of admiration, however, lies to the east. This rectangular basin, whose vertical walls are still intact, measures some 220 meters long by 30 meters wide and is nothing less than the world's very first wet dock! Constructed of fired brick, the dock was equipped with a wooden gate in order to keep in the water at low tide. Furthermore, the system was calculated both to withstand the pressure of the water and to avoid silting up. The technical prowess involved was unrivaled in the ancient world. And the

Lothal was nicknamed the "mound of the dead" after being abandoned around 1900 B.C.

game was certainly worth the candle for Lothal—the "mound of the dead" as it became known after it was abandoned—was a trading crossroads that knew no frontiers. Boats were continually plying between Lothal and Arabia, Mesopotamia and Egypt. Exports of cotton fabric, ivory, and, above all, pearls, in which Lothal excelled, as does the coastal town of Khambhat today, were traded for imports of wool and copper (which the city's craftsmen fashioned into jewelry and tools). In addition to more than fifty thousand pearls discovered on the site during the course of the excavations, archaeologists have also found a graduated circle that might well have been an ancestor of the compass and countless wax stamps used to mark the merchandise.

Now completely landlocked, the port of Lothal is one of the oldest cities, dating from India's prehistoric era. It looks as if it is going to have a rival, however, for thirty kilometers away, in the same gulf, scientists have discovered the submerged remains of another town that apparently dates from 7,500 B.C.

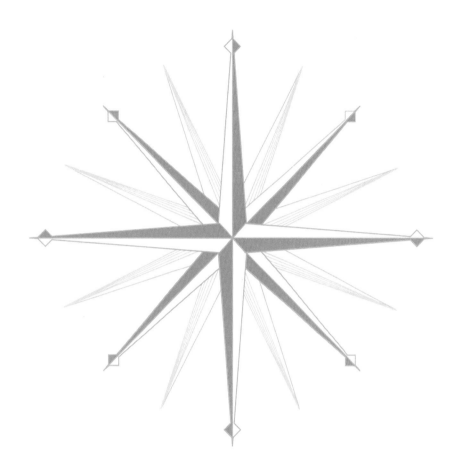

Since 1955, seven major
excavations have enabled the
history of the city,
marked by a succession of
catastrophic floods and
reconstructions, to be told

INDIA · 22°20′N, 75°25′E

MANDU
CITY OF LOVERS

Perched on the edge of the Vindhya Mountains on an isolated plateau surrounded by deep ravines, Mandu, the former capital of the state of Malwa, is one of India's largest citadels. For Indians, however, it is best known as the setting of the legendary love story involving Baz Bahadur, a Muslim prince, and Rupmati, a Hindu shepherdess with a mellifluous voice. Head over heels in love, the prince built a sumptuous palace for his beloved on the southern ledge of the plateau that overlooks the valley of his birth and through which flows the holy Narmada River. Sadly, the appetite for conquest of the Mughal emperor Akbar the Great was insatiable. In 1562 his merciless general made short work of Bahadur's small army, causing the prince to flee and leave behind his harem. Rupmati took poison in order to escape the invader's clutches. Since then, this tragic tale has inspired countless poets, painters, singers, and Bollywood scriptwriters.

Despite its romantic renown, Mandu attracts few foreigners, as it is too remote from the country's main tourist sites. Nevertheless, concealed behind its outer walls (which date from the sixth century B.C. and extend for more than forty kilometers), the fortress contains many jewels of Indo-Islamic architecture, combining Persian domes and ogee arches with the highly decorative local style. Its princes embellished the city with such a quantity of palaces, baths, mosques, mausoleums, caravanserais, gardens, and pavilions with stone moucharabies that it was nicknamed Shadiabad, the "city of happiness." But it was a city of delights of another kind, too. Tradition has it that Ghiyath al-Din, ruler of Delhi in the fourteenth century, maintained a harem of fifteen thousand wives, relatives, concubines, and servants in the Jahaz Mahal, a palace of pink sandstone that appears to float between two pools of water—to say nothing of the fearsome Ethiopian women who made up his bodyguard, provided perhaps by the same Egyptian caliphs who made the sultans a gift of several hundred small baobabs. A highly impressive sight today, these trees prosper within the precincts of Mandu, and their fruit can be bought from street vendors.

Mandu started to decline in the eighteenth century with the return of the Hindu religion and the transfer of the regional capital to Dhar. On the plateau, which metamorphoses during the summer monsoon into a vast garden sporting a thousand shades of green, the "modern" village, with its painted walls of rammed clay, its sheet metal roofs, and its stalls with precarious awnings, rubs shoulders with the ruins along the north-south road, bustling with women in brightly colored saris, rickety old trucks, and cows with painted horns. The ruins can be divided into three groups. In the center of the village, the Great Mosque, dating from the fifteenth century, is surmounted by a sea of domes. It contains a marble mausoleum that served the architects of the Taj Mahal as a template. To the north, the "royal enclave" is dominated by a pink sandstone palace. To the south, the road terminates in the love nest of Bahadur and Rupmati. At sunset, the graceful pavilion whence the beautiful Rupmati contemplated the valley spread out before her continues to attract lovers to this day.

INDORE

DHAR

MANDU

YAWAL
WILDLIFE
SANCTUARY

SYRIA · 34°32′N, 40°53′E

MARI
SUMERIAN SPLENDOR

The destiny of a city can occasionally hang on something quite trivial. This is true of Mari, the magnificent Middle Eastern capital whose identity was revealed by a simple statuette. In his book of memoirs *L'Aventure archéologique* (The archaeological adventure, 1979), André Parrot, an eminent expert on Mesopotamian civilization, describes the day in January 1934 when members of his team dug up a statuette bearing the inscription "Lamgi-Mari, King of Mari, Grand Priest of the God Enlil." This find, following the chance discovery of a Sumerian statue by some local people while digging a tomb some months earlier, removed any doubt: the Tell Hariri site was indeed Mari, one of the chief capitals of the ancient Orient, a long dreamed-of city whose history had remained a mystery for century upon century. And yet the story of this seat of the tenth dynasty reads like a novel.

Located in an arid plain traversed by the Euphrates, Mari was founded in what is now eastern Syria, a dozen kilometers from the border with Iraq, in the third millennium B.C. Having prospered on the taxes it imposed on all goods transported on the Euphrates, whose traffic it controlled, Mari dominated the region for a long period before eventually being eclipsed, most probably during the time when control of Mesopotamia was assumed by the kings of Akkad. Mari subsequently regained its former splendor thanks to powerful governors who undertook building projects on a gigantic scale, in particular the construction of a mighty brick rampart and an immense royal palace. This period from the twenty-third to the twenty-first century B.C. proved to be the city's golden age. The political metropolis also possessed considerable religious influence over the region, boasting numerous temples dedicated to the chief divinities in the Mesopotamian pantheon: Ishtar, the goddess of fertility, and Shamash, the sun god. In the nineteenth century B.C., under the Amorite dynasty, Mari started to decline as a result of the imprudent ventures of the city's last sovereign, Zimri-Lin, whose expansionist ambitions provoked the wrath of his former ally King Hammurabi of Babylon. In 1761 B.C. Hammurabi, intent on conquering the whole of Mesopotamia, ordered his troops to put Mari to the torch. It survived, but only as a humble town.

The story of this capital of the tenth dynasty after the flood reads like a novel

But for the archaeological discoveries made in the 1930s and over the subsequent years, Mari would no doubt have remained to this day a crossroads for Bedouin caravans in the middle of the Syrian Desert. Paradoxically, the discoveries owe their richness to the destruction of the city by Hammurabi's soldiers: the burning of the royal palace and most of the official buildings effectively buried precious archives and objects, including thousands of clay tablets covered

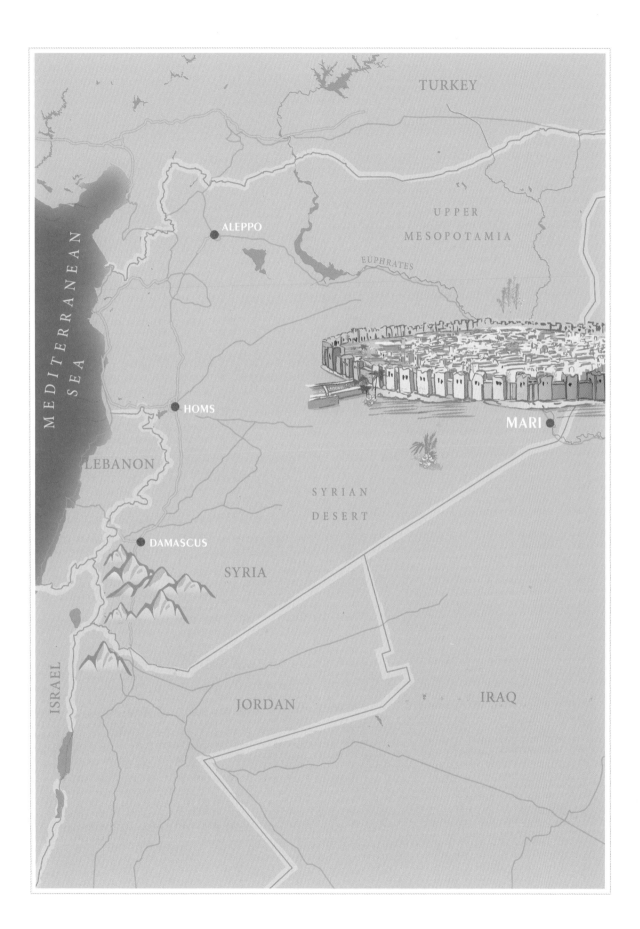

TURKEY

UPPER

MESOPOTAMIA

EUPHRATES

MEDITERRANEAN
SEA

ALEPPO

HOMS

MARI

LEBANON

SYRIAN

DESERT

DAMASCUS

SYRIA

ISRAEL

JORDAN

IRAQ

This wealth of material
that has reemerged
from the past
constitutes a treasure trove
for archeologists

with cuneiform inscriptions, under tons of rubble. Thus preserved, the wealth of material that has reemerged from the past constitutes a treasure trove for archeologists. Furthermore, it should not be forgotten that barely a fifteenth of the site (twenty hectares out of a total of 270 or more) has so far been excavated! Since the 1930s, Mari has become a key archaeological site. Everything about it is impressive: its setting, a quasi-lunar landscape that stretches as far as the eye can see, and its ruins, consisting of low walls of simple clay construction, which lead the visitor to speculate about how many kilometers of mud brick piping were required to convey water from the Euphrates to the city. Today there is not a single tree, just torrid heat and the spirit of a great lost civilization. The remains of the palace that bears the name of its last occupant, King Zimri-Lin, considered one of the most beautiful residences in the ancient Middle East, bears witness to this greatness. With its hundreds of rooms organized around courtyards, its baths and latrines, and its rooms decorated with murals, some of which can still be made out, this edifice, covering some twenty-five thousand square meters, bears testimony to Mari's former splendor. Yet the cradle of the civilization that André Parrot describes as "one of the shining lights of the ancient world" has by no means given up all its secrets. It remains to be hoped that the war that is currently ravaging Syria, accompanied by pillaging and destruction on an unknown scale at Mari and other sites, will not obliterate the "queen of the desert" all over again.

It is to be hoped that
the troubles currently ravaging
Syria and the Middle East
will not obliterate the
"queen of the desert"
all over again

MA'RIB

AT THE HEART OF THE KINGDOM OF SHEBA

Located at the center of a territory with no mapped frontiers that still belongs to Bedouin tribes, the ancient capital of the kingdom of Sheba sees hardly any tourists arrive along the road constructed in 1980 to connect it with Sana'a. The world's current troubles have rendered ancient Ma'rib, Yemen's most famous archaeological site, all but inaccessible to enthusiasts of old stones. This remote corner of the desert has nevertheless experienced an incredible metamorphosis since the 1980s, when petroleum was discovered here and a new dam was inaugurated. Today, wheat fields, orange groves, and a new, fast-growing town have sprung up around the former Bedouin village.

The story of latter-day Ma'rib seems to mirror the history of the ancient capital of the kingdom of Sheba. Founded in the western part of present-day Yemen, where rain is almost unknown, ancient Ma'rib had been inhabited since time immemorial. Its people were able to grow crops thanks to the wadis, the watercourses that gush down from the mountains before dissipating in the sands. Indeed the ancient city owes its existence to Wadi Adhana, one of the biggest watercourses in the region. In the eighth century B.C., a dam was constructed, enabling the irrigation of the surrounding fields. For more than a millennium, Ma'rib, numbering forty thousand or so inhabitants, remained a favorite halt of caravanners on the Incense Road, who liked to rest in the shade of its palm groves. Encircled by ramparts that enabled the city to defend itself against the appetites of rival states over the course of the centuries, Ma'rib was

also able to resist the Romans, who penetrated into southern Arabia in 25 B.C. Around the second century A.D., mountain tribes succeeded in taking the city, which by this time had fallen into decline as a result of the maritime routes taking traffic away from the Incense Road. By the fifth century, when the Sabaean kingdom collapsed, Ma'rib was nothing more than a small township. In the absence of any central power capable of maintaining it, the Ma'rib dam was breached a number of times before being swept away for good in 570. This marked the end of the ancient capital.

Old Ma'rib lay abandoned in the desert for fourteen centuries until its rediscovery by archaeological expeditions in the nineteenth century. However, this spot identified beyond doubt as the cradle of southern Arabian culture has been excavated only once, in 1951! In 1960, civil war bombardment made a more effective job of destroying the remains than time alone had. Perched on the brow of a small hill, the vestiges of the city deserve to be better looked after: the rammed clay walls are extremely fragile, as are the columns of the temple of Bilqis, now missing their capitals. Set into the walls at various points are stones bearing inscriptions in the Sabaean language, which local children are proud to point out to the rare visitors to the site, scant vestiges indeed of what was once the heart of a powerful kingdom. Having brought fresh life to the Ma'rib gardens with the construction of the new dam, perhaps the Yemeni regime will one day consider restoring the old stones of the erstwhile capital of the kingdom of Sheba.

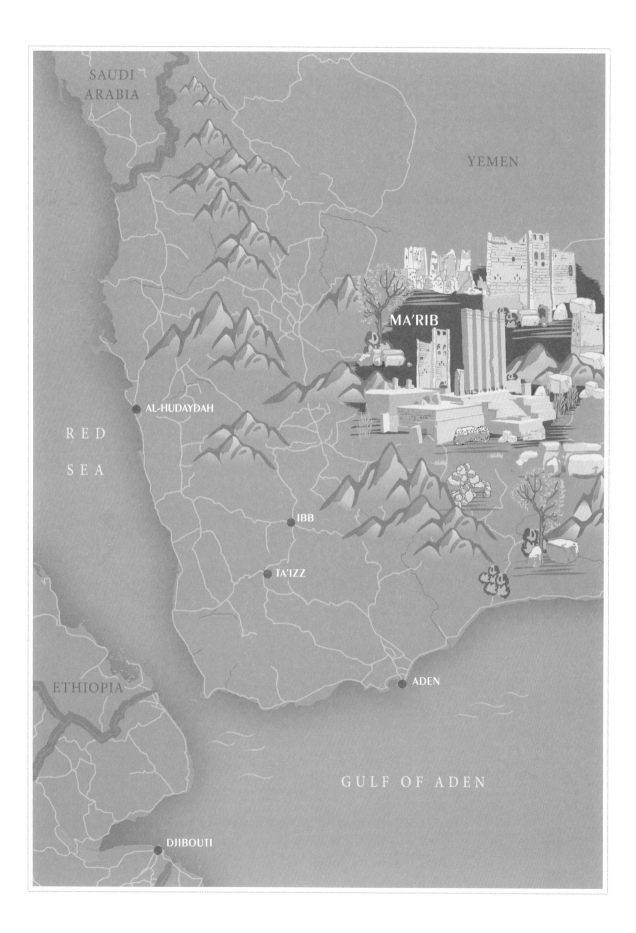

ISRAEL · 32°41′N, 35°36′E

MASADA
"... SHALL NOT FALL AGAIN"

Imposing ruins stand in splendid isolation against the backdrop of the Judaean Desert and the Dead Sea. To watch the sun rise over Masada after climbing one of the footpaths that lead up to the summit is pure enchantment. Remarkably well preserved, the fortress is equally impressive for its remains and its history. For numbers of young Israelis today, it symbolizes resistance to oppression and Israel's struggle to survive after 1948—as embodied in the popular expression "Masada shall not fall again."

Its history is instructive. This fortress atop a sheer-sided cliff some 450 meters high was built by Herod the Great between 37 and 15 B.C. Appointed king of Judaea by the Romans, Herod was loathed by his Jewish subjects and planned Masada as a refuge to which he could retreat in the event of a domestic rebellion or an invasion by Egypt. He was not a man to do things by halves: double ramparts some 1,400 meters in length encircled the plateau, a private residence whose sumptuous remains still have the capacity to astound visitors two thousand years later was built at the northern tip of the promontory, and a vast palace covering some four thousand square meters housed administrative areas, luxurious apartments, workshops, and an armory. Herod also equipped the site with watchtowers, billets for his soldiers, stables, and warehouses

To watch the sun rise over the imposing ruins of Masada is pure enchantment

abundantly stocked with jars of oil, wine, and grain—enough supplies to see the occupants through a long siege. Finally, in order to supplement the plateau's one natural spring, Herod ordered the digging of nine gigantic reservoirs, along with the construction of the necessary ducting, in order to collect as much of the precious annual rains as possible and thus safeguard the fortress from a water shortage.

In 4 B.C., Herod died without ever having occupied his refuge. Abandoned by the Roman forces, in A.D. 66, at the beginning of the Great Revolt against the Romans, Masada was used as a refuge by several hundred rebels. They were soon joined by a number of Zealots and their families fleeing the holy city. In A.D. 73, the Romans, furious at having failed in their attempt to take Masada, decided to lay siege to the fortress. The Jewish historian Flavius Josephus left a detailed account of the rebellion and the fall of the stronghold. He tells of the eight thousand legionnaires assembled at the foot of the fortress, compared to fewer than one thousand rebels defending it, of their encampment (the outlines of which are still visible in the surface of the desert), and even of the siege ramp built to support an enormous battering ram. The fortress was reconstructed in the US television series *Masada* (1980), which gives an account of how

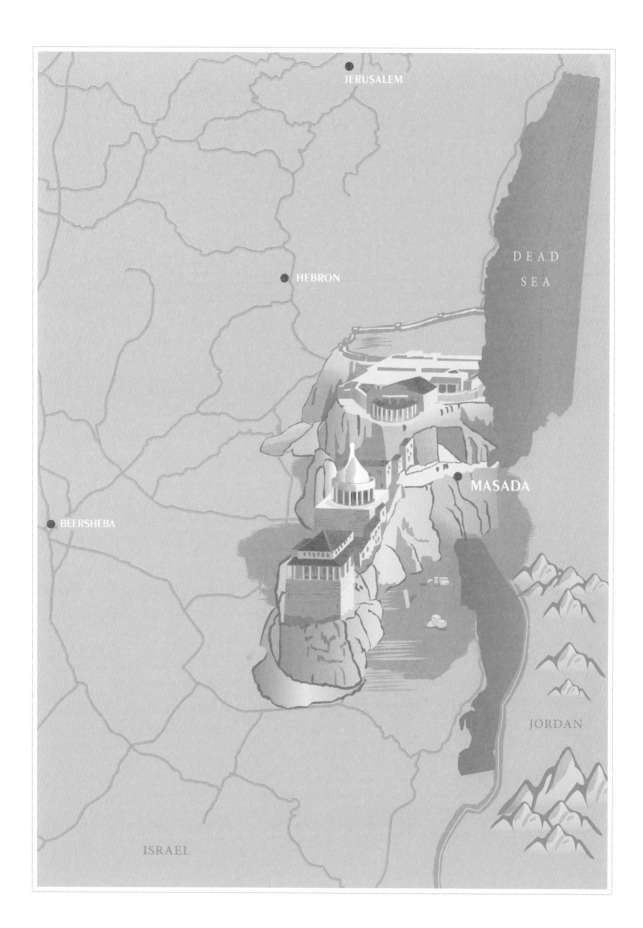

JERUSALEM

DEAD

SEA

HEBRON

MASADA

BEERSHEBA

JORDAN

ISRAEL

demoralized the Roman forces were by thirst, heat—in one of the most torrid places on earth—and sandstorms, misfortunes that also dogged the filming of the series! *Masada* also depicts the construction of the ramp by Hebrew prisoners (in keeping with the traditional account), because the Romans believed the patriotic Jews would not be able to bring themselves to kill them.

The dénouement of the siege of Masada was particularly tragic. When the Roman forces entered the fortress, they found only burned-out buildings. The historian Josephus explains that in order to deny the Romans the satisfaction of defeating them, the besieged rebels committed mass suicide after setting the main structures ablaze. Over the course of time, Josephus's account of the events inspired numerous explorers to go in search of the mythical fortress. It was finally identified in 1842, although excavations were not undertaken until 1960. Because the site had been occupied since the time of the siege only by monks (during the Byzantine era), these excavations yielded numerous exciting finds. Within the fire-damaged walls the researchers discovered thousands of everyday objects, including utensils, money, parchments, mosaics, and shards of pottery bearing individual names, among others that of Eleazar ben Ya'ir, the head of the rebels. This discovery corroborates one theory that the collective suicide was conducted via the drawing of lots, although the almost too precise correlation between historical account and archaeological finds has given rise to some controversy among the experts. There is one point, however, that is not controversial in the slightest: tourists, schoolchildren on educational outings, and Israel Defense Forces members attending their swearing-in ceremony on Masada are inevitably struck by the austere beauty of these golden brown stones spared by time, stones that embody the founding myth of the Hebrew state.

> *The besieged rebels committed mass suicide in order to deny the Romans the satisfaction of defeating them*

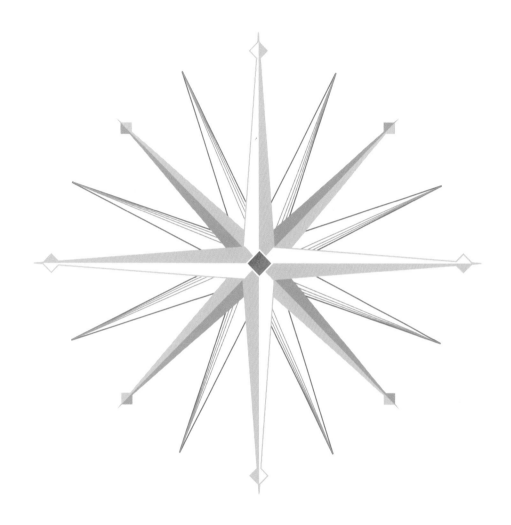

*The fortress of Masada
symbolizes Israel's struggle
to survive and its resistance
to oppression*

SANZHI
NO FUTURE

If ever aliens have touched down on planet Earth, it must have been here, at the northern tip of the island of Taiwan on the shores of the Pacific Ocean. They even seem to have left behind two bases for their flying saucers! In reality, these two villages, which sprang up some forty kilometers apart in 1978, owe their existence to a group of entrepreneurs smitten with the futuristic design of the 1970s, the decade of the Tulip chair and the Courrèges "space age" dress.

These two new towns were designed as luxury vacation resorts aimed at the Taiwanese middle classes and the US troops stationed on the island. The Sanzhi development, sitting just above the beach some fifteen kilometers from Taipei on the western coast, consisted of fifteen or so clusters of six "UFO" homes in acid colors—yellow, green, blue, pink, and orange—like giant M&Ms piled one on top of the other around a communal central staircase. Furnished with large bay windows that looked out across the ocean, the units were arranged around lush gardens whose swimming pools, equipped with toys and slides, should have been ringing with the sound of children's voices. Inaugurated in 1978, the project was canceled two years later, prior to completion. The main reasons were the departure of the US Marines in 1979 and the bankruptcy of the developer, a plastics manufacturer, in the wake of the petroleum crisis. There was perhaps another factor: the materials employed, a molded polyester and fiberglass skin over a carcass of reinforced concrete, were completely unsuited to both scorching summers and cold winters and inappropriate in seismically unstable conditions, and would have contributed little to the longevity of the new township. Mystified by the rapidly deteriorating comic book architecture, the Taiwanese spun a thousand far more appealing legends around a reality that was just a little too pragmatic: a sequence of unexplained deaths—or, better still, murders—among the workers, the presence underground of twenty thousand (!) corpses of Dutchmen killed in the seventeenth century, when the island was first colonized. In the opinion of all, however, the place was haunted, and the presence of the spirits prevented anyone from intervening to stop the site decaying into a sorry pile of rubble.

That leaves the second village, at Wanli on the east coast. Lying neglected at the foot of a development of US-style high-rise hotels, the site consists of a hundred or so of Matti Suuronen's famous capsules, which had been the main inspiration for Sanzhi. In 1968 the Finnish designer had created two models: the circular Futuro, with a ring of round portholes, four feet, and an airplane-style trap door, and the Venturo, a flattened cube glazed on each of its four sides. These houses of the future were fully fitted out, designed for all types of terrain, and capable of being dismantled and transported by helicopter. Needless to say, the residential park at Wanli had little more commercial success than that at Sanzhi. Any visitors to the site will find themselves wandering alone around these dilapidated kitschy bungalows surrounded by rampant vegetation. But wait, some of the homes appear to be inhabited—dare one hope by occupants nostalgic for this futuristic habitat dating from the 1970s?

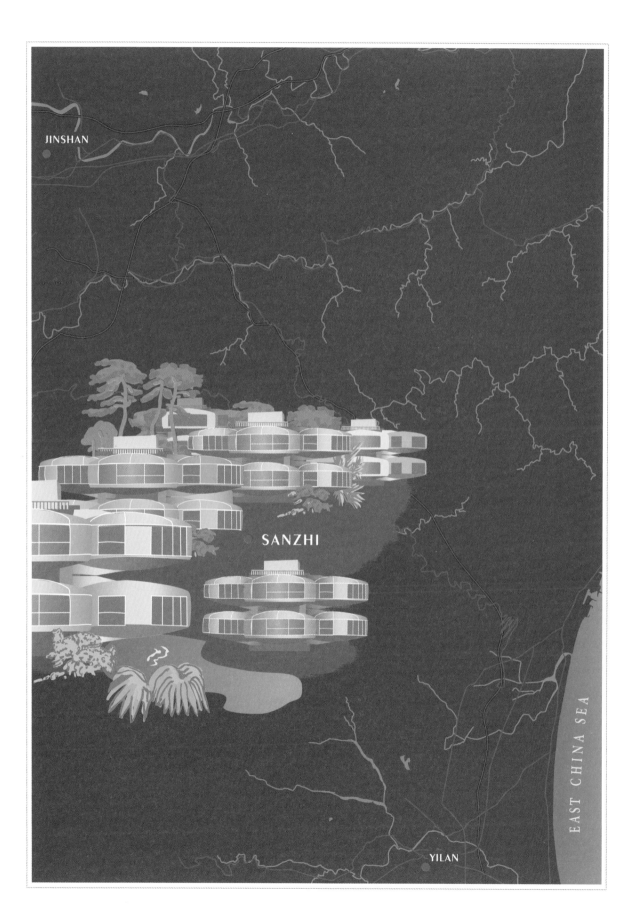

JINSHAN

SANZHI

YILAN

EAST CHINA SEA

CHINA · 29°36′N, 118°59′E

SHI CHENG
THE CHINESE ATLANTIS

The loss of Shi Cheng bears a sad resemblance to that of every other city drowned for the sake of a dam: in France the village of Tignes was submerged in 1952 to make way for Chevril dam and lake, and in Turkey the historic town of Hasankeyf is fighting to prevent itself being sacrificed so that a new barrage on the Tigris can go ahead. Although these stories have much in common, the submerging of the ancient city of Shi Cheng is unusual in that it has not prevented a revival of the city's fortunes.

In 1959 Chinese authorities completed the construction of a hydroelectric power station on the banks of the River Xin'an. To serve as its reservoir, they created the artificial Qiandao (Thousand Island) Lake at the foot of Mount Wu Shi, which happened to be the site of two magnificent ancient cities: He Cheng and Shi Cheng, built under the Han and Tang dynasties. With no qualms whatsoever, the government allowed the remains, dating back more than two thousand years, to disappear under water. Other, more recent towns and villages were also submerged, as well as almost fifty thousand hectares of agricultural land. In total, nearly three hundred thousand people were displaced.

Nothing was heard of the historic cities for more than forty years—that is, until a local official decided to make the valley, which is close to the metropolis of Hangzhou, a tourist area. The idea was a good one, as the artificial lake is surrounded by idyllic scenery, including a lush forest. Covering some 573 square kilometers and dotted with islands of all sizes, the lake soon started to attract water sports enthusiasts. In 2001, a group of divers set out to explore the crystal-clear water and discovered, to their amazement, the remains of the ancient cities at a depth of between twenty-six and forty meters. Constructed of brick and stone, the sites were incredibly well preserved, particularly Shi Cheng, the "city of lions," which presented the astounded divers with the sight of entire sections of wall decorated with sculptures, tracery, fantastical animals, and flowers. Slowly but surely, Thousand Island Lake became a diving site whose name was known all over the world. In 2004, a forty-eight-seat submarine was constructed with the aim of taking tourists and amateur explorers down to view the ruins, although it never came into operation as the use of such vessels in inland waters is prohibited under Chinese law. The site managers also fear that the turbulence around the ruins could cause damage.

Today the government is looking again at how to exploit the submerged wonders. But this means they are subject to tighter and tighter controls, and access has now been denied to unaccompanied divers. There do not seem to be any easily implementable solutions, and there is no guarantee that divers will have the right to explore Shi Cheng and He Cheng in the years to come. Perhaps the two cities will slumber forever in the silence and half-light tens of meters below the surface.

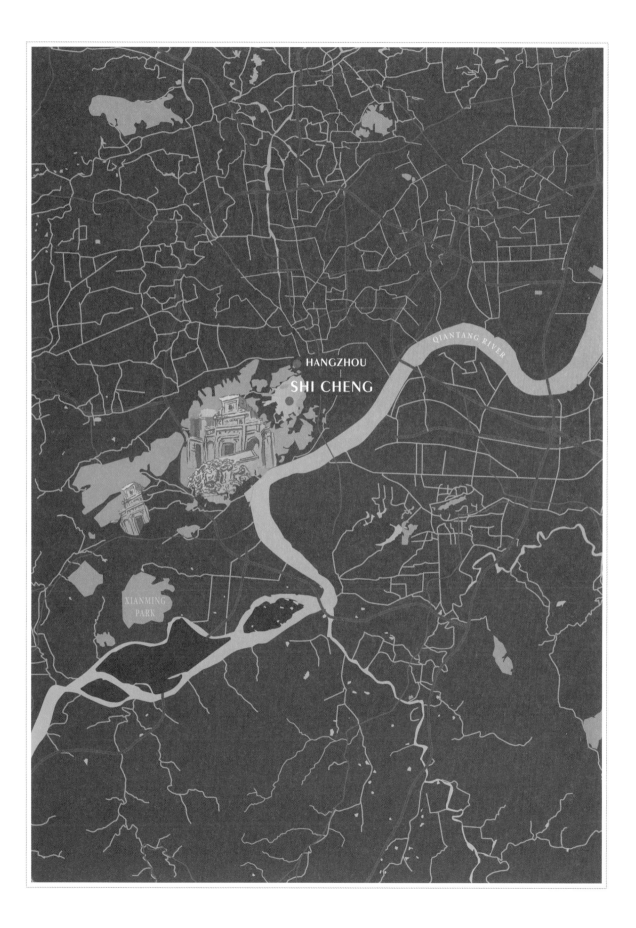

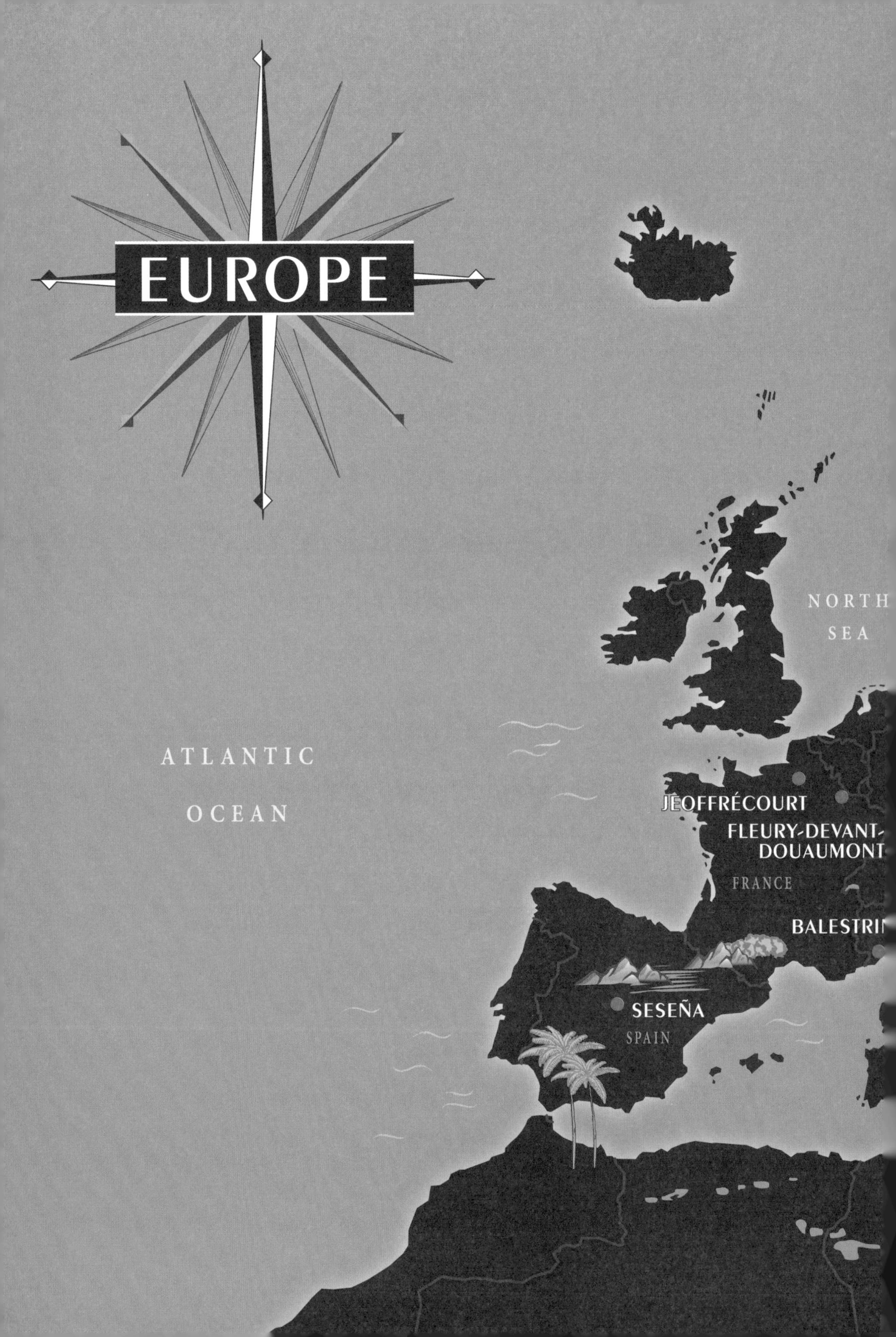

EUROPE

NORTH
SEA

ATLANTIC

OCEAN

JÉOFFRÉCOURT
FLEURY-DEVANT-
DOUAUMONT

FRANCE

BALESTRIN

SESEÑA
SPAIN

COLESBUKTA

NORWAY

BALTIC SEA

PRORA

GERMANY

PRIPYAT

UKRAINE

CASPIAN SEA

BLACK SEA

POMPEII

ITALY

VAROSHA

CYPRUS

MEDITERRANEAN SEA

ITALY · 44°07′N, 08°10′E

BALESTRINO
A SLEEPING BEAUTY

The region of Liguria has no shortage of medieval cities. From a distance, Balestrino bears a close resemblance to its neighbors. Perched at the top of a verdant hill, the town's tall stone houses cluster around the foot of an ancient castle. The bell tower of its church is visible above the pink tiles patinated by the sun, and the remains of the city ramparts bear witness to a thousand years of history. Upon reaching the first houses, however, visitors are seized by a troubling realization. There are gaping holes where windows should be, wild grass is sprouting between the wobbly paving stones, and the remains of rusty bicycles are scattered on the ground. The doors seem to have been only casually secured, and it is easy to enter the buildings. Vaulted ceilings, wide stone staircases, and festooned balconies give a hint of bygone splendor. The most desolate sight, however, is the interior of the church, with its empty niches and frescoes damaged by humidity. It is difficult to believe that this was once the economic capital of a sun-drenched valley whose prosperity was built on the cultivation of olives and vegetables.

Balestrino owes its existence to a community of Benedictine monks who, having noted the richness of the soil, settled here in the ninth century and planted vine stocks. Three centuries later, a castle was built on the hilltop, and houses gradually grew up around it. Its lords controlled the region until the eighteenth century, at which time they lost their preeminence as a result of the Kingdom of Sardinia's annexation of the territory. Balestrino metamorphosed into a humble township that lived, albeit reasonably comfortably, off its olive groves, vegetable growing, and vines. Its destiny was to be cruelly shattered, however. Starting in 1960, the town's old stone houses were shaken by repeated earthquakes. Balestrino's five hundred or so inhabitants were deeply concerned by the damage caused by the tremors, the landslides, and felled buildings, but felt utterly powerless. In 1962 they had to accept the inevitable: their town was doomed to collapse and crumble down the rocky slopes of the cliff. Forced to quit their homes by the local authorities, the people of Balestrino moved to a more hospitable site a few kilometers from the foot of the hill where they had left so many memories behind.

The abandoned town has now become a somewhat morbid tourist attraction. As visitors wander the lanes, now overrun with vegetation, they occasionally encounter the odd diehard who has chosen to remain here and attempt to lead a normal life despite all the obstacles. Although studies have been commissioned to examine the feasibility of restoring the medieval town, there is no certainty that they will come to anything in an Italy that has other cultural priorities. It is also clear that beautiful Balestrino cannot look to the intrepid tourists to save it from its fate.

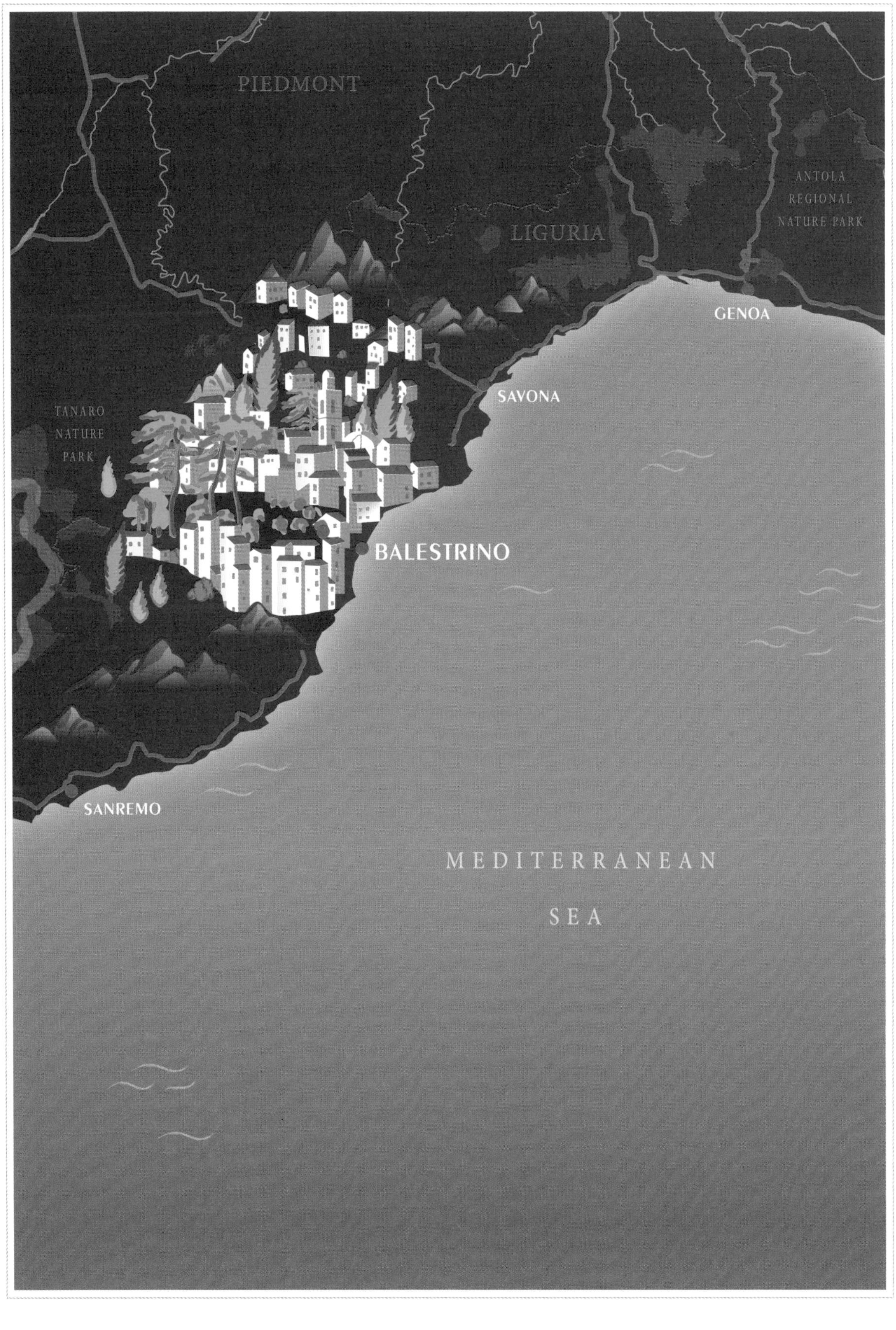

PIEDMONT

LIGURIA

ANTOLA
REGIONAL
NATURE PARK

GENOA

SAVONA

TANARO
NATURE
PARK

BALESTRINO

SANREMO

MEDITERRANEAN

SEA

NORWAY · 78°06′N, 14°58′E

COLESBUKTA
SNOW AND COAL

A t Colesbukta, located far to the north of the familiar Norway of light nights and metal-lically glinting fjords, the landscape seems timeless. The remains of this mining community tell a very unusual story. All that is left of a town that in the 1950s had 1,100 inhabitants—not an insignificant number when one stops to consider that the current population of the entire Norwegian archipelago of Svalbard is barely 2,500—are a few grayish buildings scattered along the shore of Isfjorden interspersed with rock debris and rusted metal, the vestiges of Grumant Mine.

This "bay of coal," located in an isolated spot halfway between the North Pole and the Arctic Circle, has been the setting for many an adventure. It all began in the seventeenth century, when Svalbard, discovered in 1596, became the El Dorado of whalers. With its vast, sheltered fjords, which are free of ice in winter, thanks to an effect of the Gulf Stream, this place where whales gambol proved to be an ideal hunting ground. Back then, the sea creatures were carved up on the shore and their blubber rendered in large vats. The oil commanded a high price throughout the whole of Europe and was widely used as a fuel for public lighting. This episode did

Located in an isolated spot halfway between the North Pole and the Arctic Circle, the "bay of coal" has been the setting for many an adventure

not last long, however. Within a hundred years the cetaceans had taken to the open seas, and a new chapter began.

After being occupied by—for the most part Russian—trappers in the nineteenth century, Coles-bukta's golden age dawned in the early years of the twentieth. While these trapper-adventurers had kept the Russian Empire supplied with furs, the first scientific explorers focused on the geology of the mountains along the shores of the bay, their curiosity aroused by the dark seams of coal that threaded their way between the layers of sandstone and clay. Although sailors had long been known to dig out enough of the black stuff to fuel their braziers, the idea of properly exploiting these seams did not take shape until this time, when Scandinavia was becoming industrialized. Thereupon, Colesbukta experienced a frenzy akin to the gold rush in the American West. A ferocious land grab was played out between the Norwegians, the Russians, the English, and even the Americans: the objective was to plant the national flag in a promising-looking, militarily strategic territory that had not yet been claimed by anyone else (Svalbard did not become Norwegian until 1920). In 1912, before the

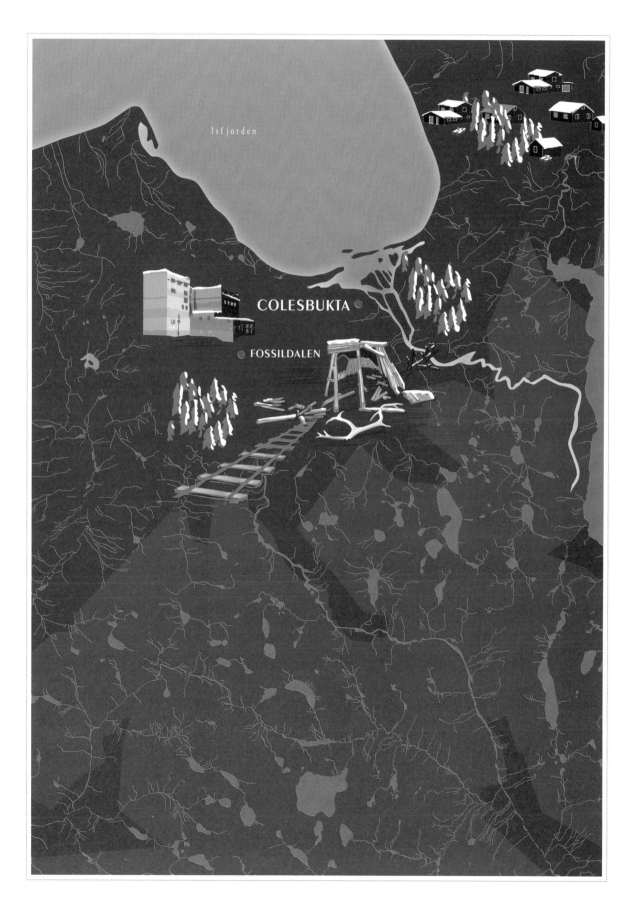

Colesbukta

is now recognized

as a site of

outstanding interest

for its flora and fauna.

Russians established themselves here, the geologist Vladimir Rusanov led an expedition to Colesbukta. A year later, operations began at Grumant Mine (the name being a Russian corruption of the word "Greenland"). The mine was active until 1941, and subsequently, with increased intensity, from 1947. It eventually closed in 1962, having become uneconomical due to its low yields.

Today, the rare visitors who venture as far as Colesbukta can still see the cabin where Vladimir Rusanov wintered before disappearing without a trace, along with his ship and crew, in the hazardous Northeast Passage. Half refuge, half self-guided museum, the cabin, with its stove and Spartan furnishings, remains the best-preserved building hereabouts.

The mine itself is located on an inaccessible shelf six kilometers to the north, identifiable from five large dilapidated shacks still standing at the site. The remains of a railroad that connected the mine to the installations in the bay area and the neighboring mine of Grumantbyen are still visible, as is a log bridge and the tunnel through which the coal was transported. In the bay area, a wooden pontoon supporting the carcass of a cabin, and the raised extremity of a loading platform some two hundred meters from the shoreline are all that is left of the harbor facilities. A scattering of buildings with their shutters closed but with their metal roofs ripped off, the gaping concrete cube of a small power station, a beached barge, and a minuscule derelict cemetery are the only reminders of the abandoned mining town in this surreal landscape in which the brilliant white ice of the mountains forms a stark contrast with the dark ground below.

Curiously, engineers have never stopped dreaming about reopening Grumant Mine, but it looks unlikely that permission will ever be granted, for the bay possesses a rare asset that promises to change the course of its history: it is now recognized as one of Svalbard's richest sites for flora and fauna. Located at the end of the world in an environment that is extremely hostile for a good part of the year, there is little chance that Colesbukta will rediscover its initial vocation. Another adventure is beginning.

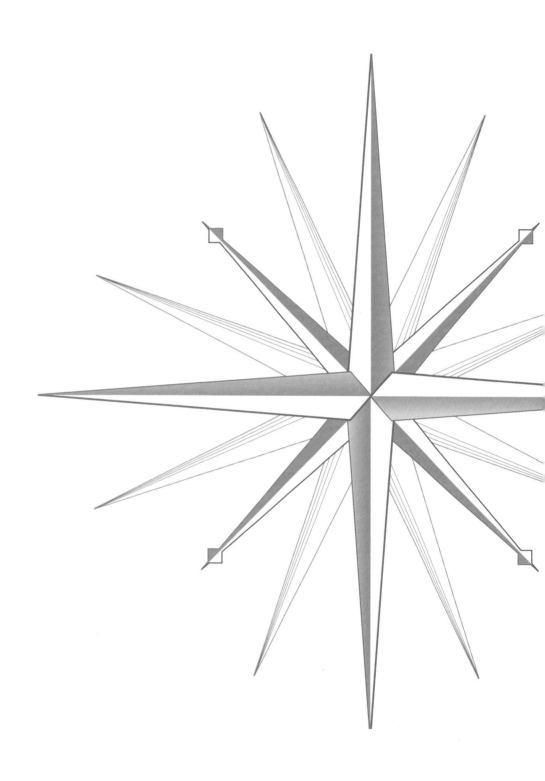

FRANCE · 49°11′N, 05°26′E

FLEURY-DEVANT-DOUAUMONT
THE VILLAGE THAT DIED FOR FRANCE

There were nine of them: nine humble peasant villages nestling in the wooded hills on the outskirts of Verdun. Nine villages obliterated forever in an unprecedented firestorm in 1916, an unutterable disaster in which Fleury-devant-Douaumont played the leading role. Until 1870, this had been a forgotten corner of France. The partial annexation of Lorraine, which effectively brought the German border thirty kilometers closer, was to change the course of its history. The fortress at Verdun had proved ineffective, and the general staff therefore decided to surround it with a double ring of defenses. This seemed like a godsend for Fleury, which received its own railroad station on the short line between Verdun and Douaumont. Until 1914, the construction of forts, redoubts, blockhouses, batteries, and depots attracted a steady flow of soldiers and laborers to the village. By the beginning of the war, only 350 souls remained in the village. Hell broke loose in February 1916 when the Germans, needing a crushing, symbolic victory, decided to launch a major assault on Verdun. As soon as the first shells were fired, the population was evacuated. On the twenty-fifth of that month, the fall of Douaumont Fort, two kilometers away, meant that Fleury was their last remaining obstacle. Between June and August it was pounded by each side in turn. The army chaplain Abbé Thellier de Poncheville describes the events in his memoirs: "The houses have been consumed by shellfire and blaze. [. . .] The fury of the fighting has dispersed everything, with shells raining down on these ruins drenched in the blood of the combatants and littered with corpses. [. . .] The location of the village of Fleury can be recognized from the color of its stones, scattered about like a mass of incessantly dispersed white spray."

The sea spray may have disappeared, but a disorderly swell of shell holes remains where the nine villages once stood. They are impossible to reconstruct because of the munitions and thousands of cadavers buried in the ground (more than sixty million shells were fired during the battle). After the war these villages were declared to have "died for France"—while retaining their virtual status as a commune. Their churches have been replaced by chapels of remembrance. Fleury's, erected in 1934, was later dedicated to Europe, whose golden stars adorn the cloak of the Virgin depicted on its façade. Where the train station once was, there now stands an instructive memorial to the victims of the monstrous battle that claimed more than three hundred thousand lives and left some four hundred thousand wounded. A little farther away is the cemetery, whose rows of tens of thousands of white crosses are splashed blood red in the summer by the dwarf rosebushes planted next to them, and the immense ossuary dominated by a lantern of the dead in the shape of an enormous shell. This is the resting place of thirteen thousand unknown soldiers. It was in front of them that Chancellor Helmut Kohl and François Mitterrand, hand in hand, solemnly sealed the new friendship between Germany and France. Although erased from the map, the name Fleury is still on people's lips: in May 2013 the remains of another twenty-six French soldiers were unearthed there.

NATIONAL
FOREST
OF VERDUN

CHARNY-
SUR-MEUSE

FLEURY-DEVANT-
DOUAUMONT

VERDUN

LORRAINE

JEOFFRECOURT
VIRTUAL CITY

Life in Jeoffrecourt, a small Picardy town located in the department of Aisne some twenty kilometers east of Laon, can hardly be described as a long, peacefully flowing river. Here the gun holds sway; armored vehicles and soldiers bristling with weaponry can regularly be seen on the streets, where fierce battles are the order of the day. The events that take place here cannot be read about in any newspaper, however. How, then, do the town's five thousand inhabitants—the customers of supermarkets, the owners of the little gray-roofed houses in the center of town, the tenants in the five-story apartment blocks, and the congregation of the "place of worship," which is no more a church than it is a mosque—cope? There is no sign of these residents. In fact, the population, along with everything else here, is virtual. The river stops dead after about eight hundred meters, the railroad barely leaves the station, the tombs in the cemetery are all anonymous, and the traffic circles around the edge of town lead off into open land, sparse woods, and thick coppices: the whole built-up area is a sham.

Most of us will never be granted access to this place, for Jeoffrecourt was designed solely for military exercises. Constructed within the Sissonne military base, which was renamed the Centre d'Entraînement aux Actions en Zone Urbaine, or CENZUB for short, it was destined to become Europe's largest training center for urban warfare, which, according to military strategists, is set to dominate most of the conflicts of the future. Possessing a fake RV park, labyrinthine shantytown, and a former munitions depot, not to forget the village of Beauséjour, several hundred meters from the town center, where sixty or so roofless buildings allow instructors to evaluate the maneuvers of their trainees from above, Jeoffrecourt receives about ten thousand recruits each year. One to two hundred soldiers based at the training center "play" opposite them, taking the role of civilians, enemy troops, or guerilla fighters as required.

The camp also includes a section of the Hunding Line, one of the defensive positions established by the German rearguard in 1916. Crossing through the site from side to side, this still has a hundred or so concrete shelters dotted along its double line of trenches.

Another reminder of the—this time very distant—past are the vestiges of a Merovingian village discovered by archaeologists at the entrance to Jeoffrecourt, next to a collection of farm buildings dating from around the turn of the twentieth century that already bore this name. These remains comprise around twenty huts and, most importantly, a burial site and chapel, an exceptional find considering the date and location of the site. One piece of good news is that the French army has agreed to protect the Merovingian site as well as the dry, chalky prairie known in the Champagne region by the term *savart*, which makes up part of the camp and has been declared an outstanding natural environment. Now the tanks attacking Jeoffrecourt skirt around the snowdrop anemone, the water mudwort, and the prostrate rocket. How reassuring!

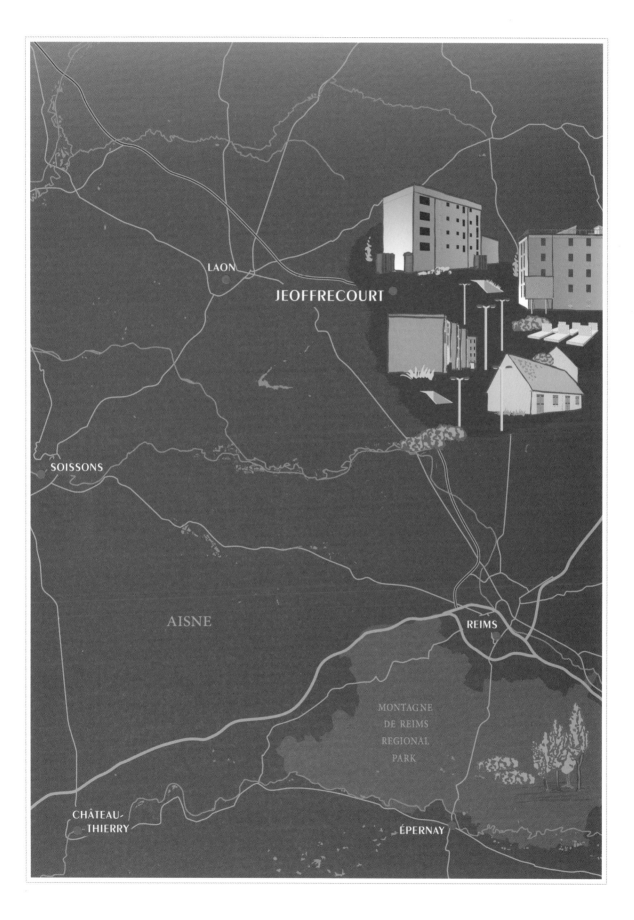

LAON

JEOFFRECOURT

SOISSONS

AISNE

REIMS

MONTAGNE
DE REIMS
REGIONAL
PARK

CHÂTEAU-
THIERRY

ÉPERNAY

ITALY · 40°45′N, 14°30′E

POMPEII

BENEATH THE VOLCANO

No lost city has ever aroused as much interest as Pompeii. Everything about its history is impressive: the scale and suddenness of the eruption that erased it from the face of the earth for seventeen centuries; the paradoxical effectiveness of the catastrophe in preserving the city over the millennia; the inexhaustible mine of discoveries that still yields treasures after two centuries of excavation; and above all the poignant presence of the victims, preserved forever in their dying postures by the burning ash, testimony to the everyday lives of Pompeians two thousand years ago. The tragic fate of the city has inspired countless works of literature and entertainment, from Edward Bulwer-Lytton's *The Last Days of Pompeii* (1834), numerous television movies, documentaries, comic books, and video games to the epic movie *Pompeii* (2014). It is even claimed that the Empire style came into fashion as a result of the initial excavations undertaken at Pompeii in the middle of the eighteenth century.

The circumstances of the cataclysm that struck the city in A.D. 79 have been known from the outset. Pliny the Younger, having observed from a safe distance the events that claimed the life of his uncle, Pliny the Elder, tells the whole story: the cloud in the shape of a stone pine that cast the whole region into darkness, the ash and pumice that rained down on the city, the

Pompeii's tragic destiny has inspired countless works of art and entertainment

shouts of alarm, the calls for help, the collapsing buildings. As new discoveries have been made and the state of archaeology has advanced, it has been possible to reconstruct the precise sequence of events of the eruption: the initial fatalities as a result of being crushed or asphyxiated by the lapilli falling from the sky, and the later wave of deaths of citizens who believed they had escaped but were stopped in their tracks by the suffocating pyroclastic flow—almost 1,250 corpses in total. Then there are the thousand and one details of daily life in this mercantile city that specialized in the oil and wine of Campania. The only conflicts for which the city had entered the annals were a brawl between "hooligans" that resulted in a ten-year ban on its gladiators and an earthquake that occurred in A.D. 62, causing damage that was still being repaired.

Like those of yesteryear, today's visitors are impressed by this fine example of Roman urban planning. The historic city covers forty-four hectares (twenty-two of which remain unexplored) and includes forums, temples, theaters, paved streets with raised sidewalks, humble dwellings with wooden balconies, more opulent homes famous for their incredibly fresh-looking frescoes and intact mosaics, the market and its cellars, thermal baths, latrines, thirty-five baker's shops, and thirty-six houses of ill repute

MOLISE
LAZIO
APULIA
(POUILLES)
BASILICATA
NAPLES
POMPEII
SORRENTO
SALERNO
CAMPANIA
GULF
OF
NAPLES

decorated in such a suggestive manner that they were once declared out of bounds to women! Visitors cannot but be moved by the sight of the casts of the victims—an idea thought up the archaeologist Giuseppe Fiorelli in the middle of the nineteenth century—many of which have been returned to the place from which their bones had originally been extracted from the hardened lava. A young pregnant woman, a husband and wife embracing their children, a patrician lady who had strayed into the gladiators' barracks (giving rise to the romantic myth of illicit love affairs)—all can be seen just as they were when death overcame them. Every tool, furnishing, crop, batch of freshly baked bread, graffito on the wall in vulgar Latin (hundreds of which exist, including obscene remarks, caricatures, real estate announcements, and slogans both sporting and political—elections were approaching) helps to build up a picture of everyday life in Pompeii. Researchers have been able to infer the date of the eruption (October or November rather than August, as previously believed) from the contents of storage jars and lit braziers. Others have analyzed the diet and standard of living of the

Researchers have inferred the date of the eruption based on the contents of storage jars and braziers

people of Pompeii based on an examination of the latrines and sewers.

Sadly, the financial resources devoted to the maintenance and protection of the site—not to mention its restoration—have declined as Italy has suffered under the recent financial crisis, with the result that the survival of these fragile remains is growing ever more uncertain. The two million or so visitors who travel to the site each year are now denied access to many streets and villas that have fallen into a bad or even dangerous state of repair, and various scandals involving the Neapolitan Camorra have underlined the negligence of the authorities over recent years.

In 2010, the collapse of the House of the Gladiators provoked outrage, prompting the Italian government to declare a state of emergency and seek financial support from Europe. While waiting for the work to commence, tourists gaze with astonishment at the rows of beans and tomatoes cultivated by local market gardeners in the areas of the city that remain buried—another way, perhaps, of reviving Pompeii.

The financial resources
devoted to maintaining the site
have dwindled, leaving
the remains of Pompeii
in an increasingly fragile state

GERMANY · 54°26′N, 13°34′E

PRORA
NAZI BEACH RESORT

This long line of apartments stretches along the east coast of Rügen, a German island in the Baltic Sea, for 4.5 kilometers. It is hard to imagine that the scrubby vegetation growing around its feet has ever been trimmed. These sinister concrete blocks with gaping windows, bearing more than a passing resemblance to a prison, are the remains of an enormous vacation complex dreamed up by Hitler's officials as a way of rewarding the model workers of the Third Reich!

Given the task of structuring the free time and leisure activities of the German labor force, the Strength Through Joy organization was ordered to build five beach resorts. Work started on the construction of the "Colossus of Prora," with the involvement of some of the most important enterprises of the day, in 1936. The ambitions of the Third Reich for the Rügen resort were boundless: Prora was to be the largest resort in the world, and its eight identical five-story blocks were to receive several million vacationers per year. In itself, the desire of Hitler's lieutenants to enable each of the country's workers to have a vacation by the sea was laudable. But these vacations were intended to play an important part in the Nazi social project. Although the plans included swimming pools, cinemas, and restaurants (which never saw the light of day), the apartments were unfailingly austere: there were communal bathrooms on each floor and the small rooms (five by two and a half meters) were all identical and lacking in decoration other than a loudspeaker through which the occupant could receive propaganda messages.

In 1939, the opening of Prora was interrupted by the start of the Second World War. The complex was never to receive a single vacationer under Hitler, and the four other planned resorts were never even built. In 1944 the buildings were converted into a military hospital, where wounded members of the Wehrmacht were treated, and also accommodated evacuees from Hamburg when that city was bombed. In 1945, Prora found itself in the territory of the communist German Democratic Republic and housed soldiers of the Red Army before being transformed into a domestic military base and, later, serving as a barracks for parachutists and a holding center for conscientious objectors. In 1990, this gigantic relic from the days of Nazi Germany was finally abandoned to nature. Since 2000, however, there has been a succession of redevelopment plans. For a while it looked as if the complex was going to be turned into luxury apartments, and a scheme to create a four-hundred-room youth hostel was eventually realized in 2014. "The largest youth hostel in Europe," announced the mayor of Binz, a neighboring town that has been welcoming vacationers since the end of the nineteenth century. If the redevelopment of the site continues, might the complex one day be allowed to forget its burdensome past? There is no doubt that Prora's Nazi origins weigh on its future, even if its classification as a historical building has safeguarded it from demolition. It is perhaps worth remembering that the plans were awarded the Grand Prix d'Architecture at the Paris International Exposition in 1937.

UKRAINE · 51°23′N, 30°06′E

PRIPYAT
A NUCLEAR POMPEII

It is a form of tourism in dubious taste to say the least, but there is a demand for it. In 2011 the Ukrainian authorities opened up the exclusion zone around Chernobyl to tourists. Within a radius of thirty kilometers around the ill-fated nuclear power plant, it is impossible to count the number of foreigners who have exchanged their highly sought-after foreign currency for permits enabling them to step foot on the site. And yet until March 11, 2011, when the incident at Fukushima in Japan occurred, Chernobyl remained the site of the most serious nuclear reactor disaster the world had ever seen. Small groups of foolhardy sensation seekers are led by guides through the accessible areas of the plant, where teams work on an ongoing basis to ensure its safety. They then climb aboard a bus for a tour through the exclusion zone. After visiting the town of Chernobyl, where a number of apartment blocks have been decontaminated in order to accommodate the technicians, the tourists are taken to Pripyat, three kilometers to the north. Everything about this abandoned city, designed by urban planners in a glorious modernist style during the heyday of Soviet socialism, seems odd. It was built in the 1960s to accommodate the power plant workers—in conditions that would have been the envy of many of their compatriots.

Everything about this abandoned city, designed by urban planners in a glorious modernist style during the heyday of Soviet socialism, seems odd

Its history came to an end on April 27, 1986. That day, the day after reactor number four exploded, the city's fifty thousand inhabitants, whom the panicking authorities had failed to inform about the catastrophe, thereby exposing them to massive doses of radiation, witnessed the arrival in Pripyat of tanks escorting a long procession of 1,250 buses. These had been chartered to empty the city of its people as rapidly as possible. The instructions were clear and irrevocable: nobody was to take anything with them because they would be returning in three days' time. The convoy of buses, stretched out over some twenty kilometers, set off on its journey out of Pripyat. The evacuees were never to return.

Today, visitors to the city are met by a deathly silence. Once their visit is over, they are forced to pass through a security gate that measures radiation. This is because in Pripyat, where no decontamination has ever been undertaken, radioactive particles in some cases reach seventy times the internationally acknowledged safe level, although the readings fluctuate according to the meteorological conditions. How to describe this "afterworld," which a number of video games, inspired by Pripyat, have tried to imagine? It is all the more chilling, perhaps, that there is nothing in the atmosphere to indicate

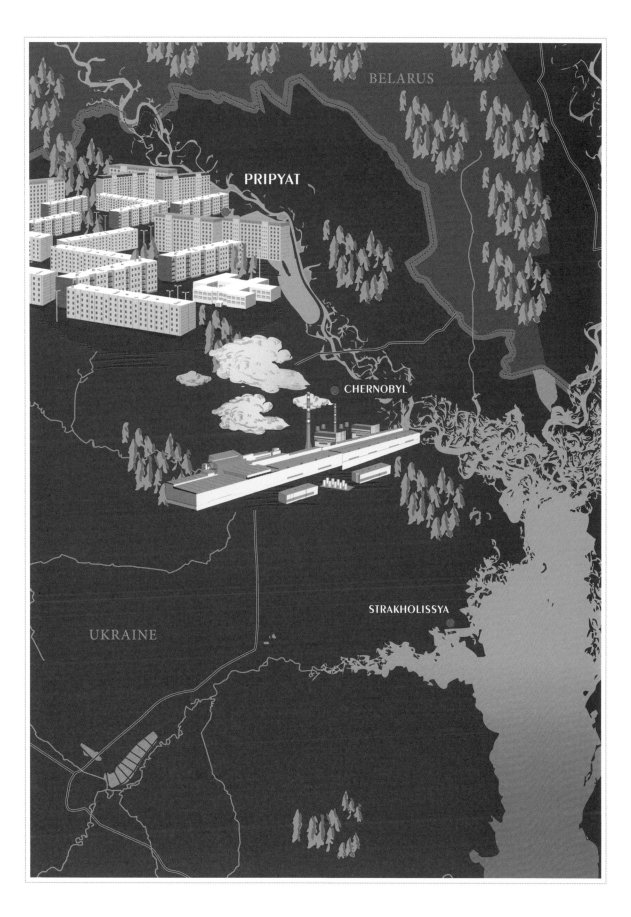

BELARUS

PRIPYAT

CHERNOBYL

STRAKHOLISSYA

UKRAINE

The award for

the most pathetic sight of all,

however, goes to

the amusement park

with its rusted equipment

that never got to be used

because it wasn't due

to open until spring 1986

the presence of danger, and one imagines that any uninformed visitors wandering between the apartment blocks separated by squares and children's play areas might well become indignant at the wastefulness of it all. What is the explanation for all these apartments with gaping windows, inside which clothing and children's toys are strewn about as if abandoned in haste? Why this swimming pool where a useless diving board overhangs a large void? Why this schoolroom where looters, outsmarting the security patrols, have scattered gas masks (cruel irony!) they found in a cupboard? The same desolate scenes are to be found everywhere, from the Palace of Culture, a vast complex that once housed a library, a theater, a gymnasium, and a conference hall, to the city's largest hotel, the Polyssia; from the hospital, where baby baskets and metal bedsteads are heaped up, to the supermarket, where cash registers, resembling robots, are still in place. The award for the most pathetic sight of all, however, goes to the amusement park, with its rusted equipment that never got to be used because the facility was not due to open until spring 1986. In the distance, the outline of the power plant can be made out, simultaneously menacing and familiar. Life stopped as the result of a technological apocalypse that nature, come spring, almost contemptuously ignores—as demonstrated by all the animals that proliferate in this zone marked forever by human negligence.

PRIPYAT
RETURN TO NATURE

Like war, nuclear disasters, a consequence of mankind's scientific and technical progress, attest to the violence of humanity and reveal the fragility of our world. Now haunted by their tragedies, some cities ruined in a matter of seconds by nuclear catastrophes have returned to nature. So it is with Pripyat and Fukushima, which have little chance of becoming habitable again for many decades to come. Unlike cities that disappeared in ancient times or as the result of industrial revolutions, there is in these two places neither poetry nor beauty; indeed, there is nothing but the memory of an almighty disaster. On the other hand, while the ground of these cities conceals an insidious poison, other cities, such as Hiroshima and Nagasaki, have been completely rebuilt, leaving to museums and commemorative monuments the task of remembering the fatal bombings. The earth possesses untiring patience in its cycle of perpetual rebirth.

SPAIN · 40°06′N, 03°39′W

SESEÑA
DELUSIONS OF GRANDEUR

Spain's largest, most absurd, and most high-profile ghost town is located at Seseña, at the very heart of the country, thirty-seven kilometers south of Madrid. This chimera came into being on the borders of Castilla–La Mancha, the scene of Don Quixote's deluded escapades. It is an architectural folly born of boundless megalomania and the frantic real estate speculation that took hold of Spain between 1999 and 2008. The development was to be called El Quiñon, after the area of fields and scrubland where it was hastily constructed between 2003 and 2008, a no-man's-land trapped between two branches of the freeway leading south from Madrid. The developer, Francisco Hernando, had this name affixed in large letters to each side of the monument in the middle of the traffic circle that is the starting point of the city's main road. At the opposite end of town, and equidistant from the park named after his wife, Maria Audena, the businessman has erected a statue of his parents. Better known in his own country by the nickname Paco el Pocero (Paco the sewer man), Hernando likes to tell how he started his working life unblocking sewers and went on to accumulate one of the ten largest fortunes in Spain and become the talk of the nation with his mind-boggling spending. His dream of creating the "ideal city," aimed at young residents of Madrid forced out of the city by prohibitive rents, is extravagant to say the least. Seseña is one of the largest private construction projects in Spain's history. Comprising 13,500 dwellings designed to accommodate more than forty thousand inhabitants, it is connected to the ancient town of Seseña, four kilometers away, which has a population of just fifteen thousand and includes an industrial zone and a low-rise district.

Seseña is one of the largest private construction projects in Spain's history

After several years of construction interspersed with accusations of illegal planning permits, bribery, and abuse of power, the complex was officially opened, at great expense, with a rock concert and five thousand guests, in 2007. No matter that only half the work was complete and most of the homes that had been finished lay empty. The new city had managed to attract only four thousand residents, compared to the sixteen thousand capacity of the 5,600 completed dwellings. A few months later, the real estate bubble burst, bringing the Herculean project to a sudden end. Spain's economic miracle was exposed as a mirage, and Seseña, its store window, died before it had even been born.

The dark hulk of the brick and concrete apartment blocks emerging from a landscape of commercial warehouses, depots, waste ground, and vast, empty parking lots now resembles a prison in the middle of the desert. The author Anthony Poiraudeau, who

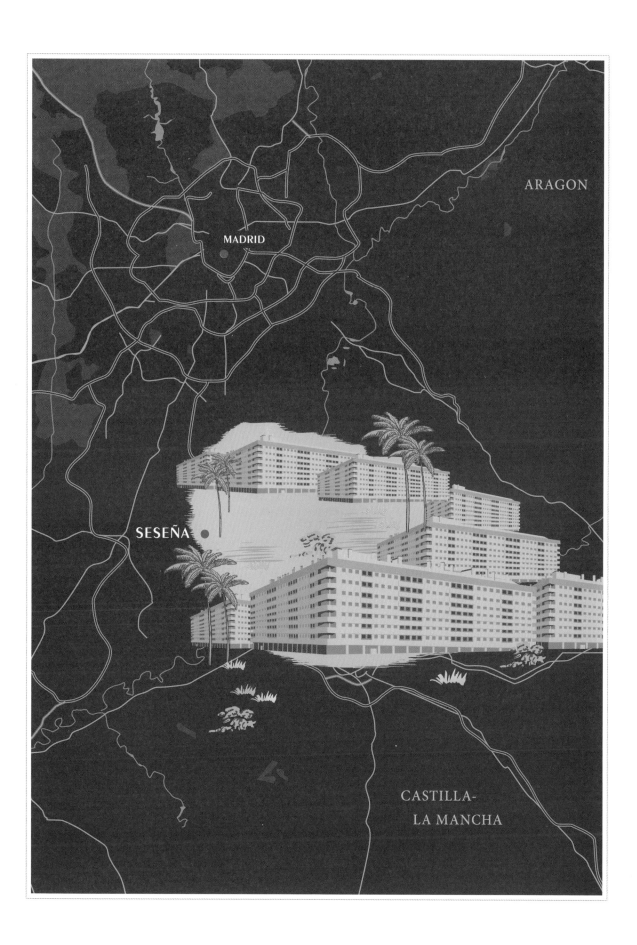

ARAGON

MADRID

SESEÑA

CASTILLA-
LA MANCHA

visited in 2012 and wrote a book about the scheme titled *The Pocero Project*, describes the city as a "hermetically sealed outpost established on a distant planet […] [in order to] test the viability there of urban life on the model of planet Earth." From one side of the development, the view is a ten-hectare tire dump; from the other, the view is of a high-voltage line that seems alarmingly close. Behind the wire fence of the unfinished construction site, along roads arranged in a grid, thirty or so apartment blocks and towers, parallelepipeds eight to ten stories high, their walls slitted with narrow balconies and almost all with their red shutters closed, form squares around concealed gardens, play and sports areas, and swimming pools. An avenue planted with palm trees, whose meager tuft of leaves offers about as much shade as a telephone pole, is trying to pretend it is a seaside promenade. No one has the slightest desire to linger here, in an incessant wind that whips up the dust on this plain,

Seseña is identical to the kind of impersonal city seen in video games

which is scorching in summer. On the ground, the outlines of unbuilt blocks are littered with abandoned materials or else have already been concreted and are bristling with iron rods. With its empty sidewalks and stores that have never opened, Seseña resembles the kind of impersonal cities seen in video games.

"FOR SALE" signs can be spotted everywhere. The banks have seized hundreds of properties from borrowers in default, but despair of being able to sell them, even at reduced prices. Having foreseen all of this, El Pocero left the city to its fate in 2009 to go in search of riches under more clement skies. In Equatorial Guinea he thought he had convinced the head of state, Teodoro Obiang, to invest massively in a complex of thirty-six thousand homes (in a country of seven hundred thousand people!). When the dictator withdrew, Hernando tried to obtain compensation from the World Bank. El Pocero is now said to be cherishing hopes of doing business with Saudi Arabia.

In this city that died
before it was even born,
"FOR SALE" signs can be seen
everywhere

CYPRUS · 35°06′N, 33°57′E

VAROSHA

FORBIDDEN ZONE

In 1972, the town proclaimed the "Jewel of Cyprus" by advertising posters had just been born. A resort district of the city of Famagusta, once an important trading and fishing port, Varosha was intended to become the island's main tourist center. While its modern concrete architecture disfigures the coastal landscape for a length of almost six kilometers, Varosha's inhabitants benefited from idyllic views of the Mediterranean. The place was a dazzling success, attracting tens of thousands of new residents, Greek and English for the most part, who rubbed shoulders with tourists seduced by its shopping malls, hotels, and many souvenir shops.

The death of this brand new beach paradise came as swiftly as its success. In 1974, the Turkish invasion of Cyprus transformed Varosha into a sinister no-man's-land. The resort had the misfortune of finding itself on the demarcation line between the southern part of the island and the self-proclaimed Turkish Republic of Northern Cyprus. Devastated by the bombardment and abandoned by its inhabitants, who fled, leaving all their possessions behind, by the time the Turkish army took control and declared Varosha a "forbidden zone," it was little more than a pile of ruins. Since then, no one other than the Turkish military has been allowed to enter what has become a ghost town. Ringed by sentry boxes and barbed wire in order to dissuade any adventurers from trying to enter the site, Varosha is literally a ghost of its former self, with the façades of its apartment blocks damaged by fire and explosions and its streets overrun with Mediterranean vegetation. Around the edges of the forbidden zone, scarlet signs deter the most foolhardy with messages that could not be more explicit, such as THE TAKING OF PHOTOGRAPHS IS FORBIDDEN and WHO ARE YOU?

Located a few meters away from the security fences, one hotel is taking advantage of the sad history of the former beach resort in its own unique way. Its management is offering either a view of the sea or a view of the ruins, and the hotel's occupancy rate is said to exceed eight-five percent all year round. Is there not something a little voyeuristic about this curiosity? Or is it merely the sight of the fine sandy beaches lining the forbidden zone that attracts visitors to this side of the hotel? One thing is certain: the Cypriots who knew Varosha during its short but attractive existence, or in some cases the village that preceded it, are hurt by this new infatuation. For them, the desolate resort represents, above all, the shame of their country, whose territorial division it symbolizes. The occupation of the north of the island by the Turkish army still divides the international community, which to this day does not recognize the Turkish Republic of Northern Cyprus. In 2008, the southern part of the island joined the European common currency union, the Eurozone, while for the time being, the northern part is excluded from the European project. There is little chance of Varosha rising from the ashes anytime soon.

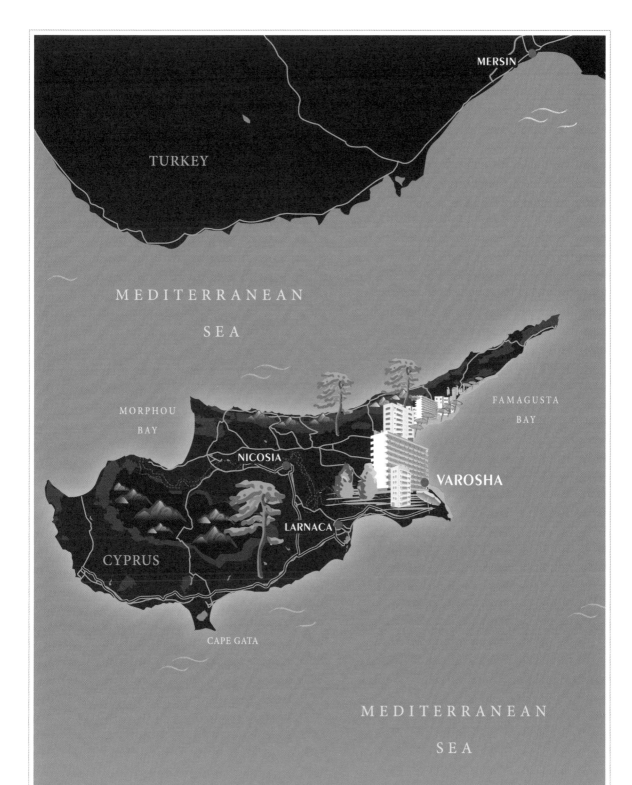